THE JUSTICE
GOD IS SEEKING

DAVID RUIS

Regal

From Gospel Light
Ventura, California, U.S.A.

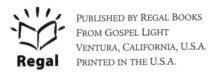

PUBLISHED BY REGAL BOOKS
FROM GOSPEL LIGHT
VENTURA, CALIFORNIA, U.S.A.
PRINTED IN THE U.S.A.

Regal Books is a ministry of Gospel Light, a Christian publisher dedicated
to serving the local church. We believe God's vision for Gospel Light is to
provide church leaders with biblical, user-friendly materials that will help
them evangelize, disciple and minister to children, youth and families.

It is our prayer that this Regal book will help you discover biblical truth
for your own life and help you meet the needs of others. May God richly
bless you.

*For a free catalog of resources from Regal Books/Gospel Light, please call your
Christian supplier or contact us at* 1-800-4-GOSPEL *or* www.regalbooks.com.

Rights for publishing this book in other languages are contracted by Gospel
Light Worldwide, the international nonprofit ministry of Gospel Light.
Gospel Light Worldwide also provides publishing and technical assistance
to international publishers dedicated to producing Sunday School and
Vacation Bible School curricula and books in the languages of the world.
For additional information, visit www.gospellightworldwide.org; write
to Gospel Light Worldwide, P.O. Box 3875, Ventura, CA 93006; or send an
e-mail to info@gospellightworldwide.org.

DEDICATION

To my new-found community in Los Angeles
and to the journey of Basileia . . .
may we ever discover the fragrance of justice.

CONTENTS

ACKNOWLEDGMENTS

Hey guys, I said I wouldn't forget ya . . .

To the Atkeys—who've risked it all again and again in the pursuit of worship and justice—you're an inspiration . . . and to the Millers—you guys rock— keep searching out those prophetic gems that bring people hope and life in the midst of the swirl of life.

Of course, I can't not mention my family— Anita—the babe, the one—thanks for being my shining example of mercy. Tams, keep looking ahead—the best is yet to come. Crystal, here's to new adventures out of the nest along the path of justice. Jael, you captivate the message of the heart like so few do—go for it girl. Josiah, run, man—run with all you've got.

Don Williams—you are a true mentor and friend . . . here's to Kingdom justice breaking into Hollywood!

Dad, Mom and Sandi . . . thanks for everything.

INTRODUCTION

The heart of the matter is this: The agenda of Jesus *is* justice.

> The scroll of the prophet Isaiah was handed to him. Unrolling it, he found the place where it is written: "The Spirit of the Lord is on me, because he has anointed me to preach good news to the poor. He has sent me to proclaim freedom for the prisoners and recovery of sight for the blind, to release the oppressed, to proclaim the year of the Lord's favor" (Luke 4:17-19).

To follow Christ is to be led here, to this place where worship and justice kiss. Just as Jesus experienced the anointing of the Holy Spirit, enabling Him to fulfill His mandate, He gives this same power and authority to all who would partner with Him in Kingdom life and ministry. When Jesus sent out His disciples on their first ministry adventure, He told them:

> As you go, preach this message: "The kingdom of heaven is near." Heal the sick, raise the dead, cleanse those who have leprosy, drive

out demons. Freely you have received, freely
give (Matt. 10:1,7-8).

And when Jesus was challenged by John the
Baptist's disciples as to the authenticity of His mes-
sianic call, He told them to relay this message to
John:

The blind receive sight, the lame walk, those
who have leprosy are cured, the deaf hear, the
dead are raised, and the good news is preached
to the poor (Matt. 11:5).

Christ's ministry took Him to the most broken
aspects of society, and it was here that His call was
authenticated. This was not just about *power* ministry,
platforms or religious performance; this was about
justice. Simply said: Things out of line with God's
kingdom rule must be set right.

Disease and sickness are out of line with Kingdom
rule: Go and set it right. Although it is appointed for
all people once to die, where death has come before its
time: Go and set it right. Touch those who are pushed
to the margins of society under the curse of "untouch-
able" diseases: Set it right. Break the back of demonic

harassment and torment in the mighty name of Jesus: Set it right. Bring the message of hope and liberty to those under oppression and stand with them against the attitudes, governments and structures that reinforce its grip: Set it right. With what has so freely been given, now generously give: Set it right. Bring the justice of the kingdom of heaven.

> Jesus went through all the towns and villages, teaching in their synagogues, preaching the good news of the kingdom and healing every disease and sickness. When he saw the crowds, he had compassion on them, because they were harassed and helpless, like sheep without a shepherd. Then he said to his disciples, "The harvest is plentiful but the workers are few. Ask the Lord of the harvest, therefore, to send out workers into his harvest field" (Matt. 9:35-38).

As followers of Jesus, we cannot ignore what moved Him to send out the first of His disciples, what moves Him still to send us out today: *compassion*. Biblical compassion is a uniquely Christian virtue. The great preacher Charles Spurgeon explained it this way:

It is expressive of the deepest emotion; a striving of the bowels—a yearning of the innermost nature with pity . . . when our Savior looked upon certain sights, those who watched Him closely perceived that His internal agitation was very great, His emotions were very deep, and then His face betrayed it, His eyes gushed like founts with tears, and you saw that His big heart was ready to burst with pity for the sorrow upon which His eyes were gazing. He was moved with compassion. His whole nature was agitated with commiseration for the sufferers before Him.[1]

To touch Christ is to touch compassion. Far beyond a guilt-trip, a tweaked conscience or a pale sense of pity, compassion reaches into the very guts and demands action. It compels prayers that will move heaven, intercessions that cry out for workers to be thrust into this weighted-down harvest. It motivates one to *move*—to go and set it right—to administer justice through the power of the Kingdom.

Real religion, the kind that passes muster before God the Father, is this: Reach out to the homeless and loveless in their plight, and guard against corruption from the godless world (Jas. 1:27, *THE MESSAGE*).

Just as the earliest followers of Jesus would never undertake this justice mandate apart from knowing the deep compassion that moved Christ, we must beg to know His compassion before we embark on the reflections in the following pages.

Jesus saw the crowds. He saw them harassed and helpless, bent low under the weight of the Roman government's domination and the unreasonable demands of the Jewish system of law. He saw them—sheep without a shepherd—and it broke Him.

Today, we have new governments with the same old agendas, lots of religion, and not much freedom. Can you see the crowds—sheep without a shepherd—today?

It broke Him.

May it break us.

It sent Him.

May it send us.

Note

1. C. H. Spurgeon, "The Compassion of Jesus." Sermon delivered Thursday, December 24, 1914, at the Metropolitan Tabernacle, Newington, England. http://www.spurgeon.org/sermons/3438.htm (accessed March 22, 2006).

CHAPTER 1

A PLACE TO BEGIN

> All appears to change when we change.
>
> HENRI-FRÉDÉRIC AMIEL

If Jesus had a business card, I think it would say, "Mess-With-Your-Mind Ministries, International." He is a master at challenging our ways of thinking by adjusting the lens through which we see. When you respond to His kingdom summons, He takes that as an invitation to start the adjustment, which can *really* mess with your mind.

At the core of His kingdom summons is this mind- and heart-altering challenge: *Repent, for the Kingdom is upon you.* To repent is to change your way of thinking—or more precisely, to change the way you *see* life. The Greek is clear: *metanoia* (repent) means to shift the way you perceive. There is an alternate reality beyond what we see through the fallen sight of our natural eyes. There is another way to live; a way higher than the one we are comfortable in or resigned to.

Just like the foreboding scene in *The Matrix* in which the challenge is made to Neo to take the red pill or the blue, so there is a decision to be made for all those who would encounter Christ and His call to Kingdom life: Swallow His words and you will never see—or *be*—the same again.

The kingdom of God is upon us, and it is on a radical collision course with the normal. Its priorities are different. Its definitions of life, love and happiness are unlike those embraced by the world. Its definitions of success and fulfillment are upside-down from the tabloid celebrities and media moguls that society lifts up as its heroes. It is completely *other*: a holiness not sustained by outward rules, regulations and religious conformity, but a way of righteous living that confronts the powers and systems of the age. Light clashes with darkness. Liberty challenges oppression in both the seen and unseen realms. Lifestyles of generosity and meekness—the embrace of weakness and the weak—fly in the face of the false promise of security on Earth with a hopeful determination to store up treasure that will be enjoyed in another time and place, beyond *here*.

As Jesus warned, this Kingdom is one that does not stand still and will not go quietly into the night. There is a violence inherent within its advancement that is not about bombs, guns and political agendas, but rather about tearing down systems of thought that exalt themselves above the ways of God, and about demolishing strongholds that blind people to the reality of the kingdom of heaven. Jesus is never more clear about the ferocity of the Kingdom than in Matthew 11:12:

> From the days of John the Baptist until now, the kingdom of heaven has been forcefully advancing, and forceful men lay hold of it.

To be a part of this Kingdom—to be birthed into it via this mind-altering repentance—is to become part of this world-altering agenda.

> For though we live in the world, we do not wage war as the world does. The weapons we fight with are not the weapons of the world. On the contrary, they have divine power to demolish strongholds. We demolish arguments and every pretension that sets itself up against the knowledge of God, and we take captive every thought to make it obedient to Christ (Col. 10:3-5).

Out of all the concepts that have challenged my worldview as a follower of Jesus, the one thing that has stretched me the most is the centrality of *justice and mercy* to the character of God and the advancement of His kingdom. I have come to believe that any expression of worship to Him lacks integrity when injustice is ignored and the love of mercy goes uncultivated. Righteousness and justice are the pillars of His throne and the foundation upon which His kingdom rests (see Pss. 89:14; 97:2; Isa. 9:7).

My Turning Point

So there I was, leaning against the back wall in the middle of a church worship gathering.

The whole concept of worship expression in church had been shifting in me for some time. I came from a conservative theological tradition and was trained as a classical musician, so the way our liturgy was heading was unlike anything I'd ever seen before. I was being stretched; and while I was discovering that I liked

> In love a throne will be established; in faithfulness a man will sit on it—one from the house of David—one who in judging seeks justice and speeds the cause of righteousness (Isa. 16:5).

the pro-cess of being changed, I still had some theological and cultural suspicions about the direction that God was leading.

As part of the team that planted the church, the role of worship leader fell to me because of my background in music (and because I needed to earn the paycheck that I was getting from the offering!). Honestly, I didn't have a clue what we were doing, but as we pursued an expression of worship that was more intimate with God and truer to our culture, something began to change in us. It was more than just a shift in musical presentation and instrumentation; our hearts were somehow softening under an ever-increasing awareness of God's presence. That awareness was stirring a love for Him that was transforming our lives and the decisions we made. Something was up.

One of the young men interning with us was leading the liturgy that day, and it was *sweet*. It was unusual for me not to have some role in the service, and I welcomed the chance to just take it all in with no public responsibility. As I was resting in the moment, a startling notion blazed across my thought patterns. I didn't hear a voice, nor did all other awareness stop, but a thought whispered in my mind like a shout above the music—a great booming voice that would change me forever.

What I heard was this: *The fragrance of worship is justice . . . where there is no justice, there is no fragrance.*

I believe the Holy Spirit was speaking to me that day. Feeling more dazed than spiritual, I was propelled into a theological and experiential journey, of which I am still very much at the beginning stages. Jesus messed with my mind, and I have not been able to *see* the same way since.

Repentance had caught up with me. I began to care about issues and people that I had not cared about before that moment. My prayers were constantly invaded by images of poverty and injustice, and my nice little myopic world was being pulled to a place of intercession that not only spilled out through my words but also started to move my feet into situations I would've never imagined before.

Beginning to *See*

Nearly every day for five years, I had driven by a block of motels near my home. In that whole time, I had never *seen* them before. Almost immediately after my mess-with-your-mind worship experience, I *saw* them. And when I saw, I could not look away.

They looked nasty. The signs said that there were not only daily and weekly rates, but that there were also monthly rates for those who chose to stay. Could it be that people actually *lived* there?

I met Betty, who *did* actually live there. She was an older woman whose husband went to get the mail a memory ago and never came back. Her world went into a downward spiral of poverty that had ended up with her in that fleabag motel: cold, hungry and alone.

I knew this wasn't about starting a ministry, firing up a program in the church, or doing a good deed to ease my conscience. *This was about the simplicity of worship.* As much as I was awakening to intimacy with Christ through a changing ethos of music and the arts, it struck me while talking with Betty that when meeting the "least of these" here in the motel at the fringe of society, I encountered Him.

I went home deeply shaken and began to process these events with my wife. At that time, we had two little kids and not much stuff. Without big fanfare, we grabbed some canned goods from our pantry and a few perishables—and most important of all, a big blanket (it was a terribly cold winter)—and started down the path of finding friends among the poor and marginalized. And in finding friendship with the poor and oppressed, we found God in a way that I would have never thought possible.

As we became friends with Betty, she eventually became a friend of God. A short time after our first meeting, she checked out of that nasty motel and went to live with Him forever. I can't wait to see her again and thank her for introducing me to what life and worship are all about.

There is a fragrance in this kind of friendship and worship that is unmatched in any other place, and if we do not make it a part of our lives, it is lost in the gathered place of liturgy. It is lost not only to the church and the culture to which it is called; it is lost to God—a tragedy indeed.

> You are the salt of the earth. But if the salt loses its saltiness, how can it be made salty again? It is no longer good for anything, except to be thrown out and trampled by men. You are the light of the world. A city on a hill cannot be hidden. Neither do people light a lamp and put it under a bowl. Instead they put it on its stand, and it gives light to everyone in the house. In the same way, let your light shine before men, that they may see your good deeds and praise your Father in heaven (Matt. 5:13-16).

As one who has a calling to serve the Church at large by making a way for her to express worship, I cannot be silent about justice. We cannot be a worshiping people aside from seeking justice within and without our walls. I cannot be faithful to my destiny in worship without wrestling continually with the place of justice in my life as a worshiper and in the life of the community in which I worship.

So this is an invitation: An invitation to simply begin. An invitation to have your mind messed with.

Beyond strategies, nonprofit organizations and giving to the cause, dare to be changed. Dare to *see*.

Repent, the Kingdom is upon you.

CHAPTER 2

THE FRAGRANCE OF JUSTICE

> As for your justice, so great is the fragrance it diffuses
> that you are called not only just but even justice itself,
> the justice that makes men just.
>
> ST. BERNARD OF CLAIRVAUX

Most times, it's the smell that gets me. I'm not sure why, but my greatest struggle is olfactory. Even after many years of friendship with people whose stench alone could hold them at the fringes of society, my gag reflex is firmly in place.

My newest adventure into relationship with the poor is in the dark shadows under a bridge at the junction of the 2 and 101 freeways on the outskirts of Hollywood. The reek of urine and other bodily emissions can be quite overpowering, and engaging in conversation here demands some serious focus to hold down my lunch. The smell of life on the street has its own signature perfume.

My earliest memories of walking with those broken on the altar of injustice involve the sense of smell. Among them are the guy from the streets as he unloaded a dump of diarrhea in the middle of a conversation; the time I crouched down in a living space at the back of a warehouse with my eyes tearing up from

the pungent intensity swirling through the brokenness; and the aftermath of a rippling fart bouncing off
the front pew in the middle of a sermon—a satisfied
grin on the face of the perpetrator and looks of shock
all around.

It's the smell that gets me.

It's the same in the places I go outside the insula-
tion of Western prosperity. Open sewage and open
sores. The mixed odors of exotic perfume and the
stench of poverty, with no middle-class buffer to keep
them apart. The stink of religion gone mad and fatal-
ism unchecked, of abuse of power and the innocents
it enslaves. The reek of desperation and decay. It's the
smell that gets me.

But here's the miracle: Just when my senses are
on overload and I don't think I can take anymore, I
sniff a sweet aroma cutting through the nausea,
and before long there is true beauty among the
ashes. There is a tantalizing fragrance that touches
the place of worship like no other. From beneath
the stale fumes of brokenness and human decay,
there is a smell I have come to love. And most sur-
prising of all, I have discovered it is a scent that
delights the nostrils of God Himself. It is the fragrance of justice.

The Fragrance of Worship

The "fragrance of worship is justice" word from the Spirit and those first simple steps toward friendship with the marginalized happened long before my life's path took me into the good, bad and ugly of the worship industry. Long before I had any published songs or had stepped into the world of recording, my compass had been divinely set toward the fusion of worship and justice. As much as the discovery of different expressions of worship would stretch me beyond my classical training, I never dreamed where it would take my theology, life and lifestyle.

It is difficult to express here how deeply grateful I am for this early understanding. It's quite plain from the biblical definition of *true* worship, but without a nudge from the Holy Spirit, I'm quite sure I would have missed it. I cannot say how much of my worship since that day has been delightful to the Lord, but I knew then as I know now that I can never remove the pursuit of justice and mercy from the equation.

After my turning point and those first stumbling steps, I toppled into a biblical study that would take me to more than 2,000 verses in the Old and New Testaments that focus on God's heart for the poor and oppressed. Everywhere I looked, I saw an imbalanced distribution of wealth and power—not just in the systems of the age, but also in the Church herself—and the resulting destruction from this disparity. I saw injustice and poverty all around me, here in the westernized world as much as in the occasional World Vision commercial, and what I saw exposed deep spiritual issues I previously thought I'd never have to contemplate.

As my theology adjusted and my heart awakened, I knew I could not remain the same. I knew that my relationship with God was due for a serious overhaul and that my understanding of worship would forever be altered. Rendering worship to God while oblivious to the suffering in the world around me became impossible and somehow distasteful. Simply put, I now saw it as *wrong*.

The Offering God Accepts

One of the first biblical passages that rocked me to the core, forever altering my concept of what it means to have integrity as a worshiper, was the penetrating word of the prophet Amos (quoting God) as he critiqued the worship of God's people:

I hate, I reject your festivals,
I will not stomach your assemblies.
Even though you offer me burnt offerings

and your grain offerings,
I won't accept them;
and the peace offerings of your prize beasts
I won't approve.
Spare me the roar of your songs;
I won't listen to the music of your guitars
(Amos 5:21-23, *Postmodern Bible*).

Yikes! Not good news for a worship musician and songwriter—or *any* worshiper, for that matter. I have yet to see a bumper sticker or key chain imprinted with these verses on display at the nearest Christian trinket store. It's not a theme that sells well.

The *New International Version* puts it this way: "Away with the noise of your songs," but the *Postmodern Bible* version quoted above captures the harsh vibe. You can almost see God rolling His eyes as He turns His head, sighing, "Oh, spare me."

Even now, reflecting as I write, I get that gnaw in the pit of my stomach when I wonder if this might be God's response to the latest song that I thought I wrote for Him. Didn't the people get into it and weren't they touched? Maybe . . . but was God into it? *Was God touched?*

There is something God is looking for beyond the activity of worship, beyond the expression alone. Detached from a lifestyle engaged in the righting of wrongs, it's all noise. Worship given that does not come from a community that cares for the poor, rejects injustice and embraces generosity turns something meant to be sweet into something very sour. It distorts a beautiful melody into something discordant and mutates even the most well-intentioned act of worship into a gift that God will not receive—a sacrifice He completely rejects. Yet we can convince ourselves that God is pleased if we do not learn to see with His eyes, hear with His ears and retune our senses to what moves and delights His heart.

All three sacrifices referred to in the Amos passage—the burnt offering, the grain offering and the peace offering—are given by free will. They are given as a voluntary and personal act of worship. This gives the warning incredible punch. God is taking issue with those who have taken an extra step in expressing their devotion to Him. These are the sacrifices of the truly dedicated, those who take their commitment very seriously and who are willing to give from a place of deep sacrifice. These offerings were meant to be pleasant and sweet-smelling to God, yet something

here is drastically off the mark.[1] The burnt offerings,
grain offerings and peace offerings were said to produce a "soothing aroma to the Lord," yet God is anything but soothed.[2]

Something is missing.

The burnt offering allowed people to actually
participate in the ceremony of the sacrifice. It was a
point of contact for people beyond the priestly
Levites who, in every other sacrificial rite, were the
only ones allowed to directly participate. This offering was a way to *personally* demonstrate the individual's love for God. It signified the complete dedication of the offerer to the Almighty, and it became
the frame of reference for New Testament worship
as described in Romans 12:1.

Yet . . . something is still missing.

The purpose of the grain offering was not atone-
ment (like the burnt offering), but simply to worship,
to acknowledge God's divine provision for the needs
of life itself. To give grain was very difficult, because
the gift came from the seed for next year's planting.
Grain offerings were given not out of necessity (as
were other offerings in the sacrificial system), but as a
sign of true devotion. Thus, the human element is present in the grain offering in a way that it is not in the

burnt offering.[3] The pleasant mix of the roasting grain and olive oil would indeed create a pleasant odor that would make the worship experience delightful.

Yet though these were brought before the Lord with sincerity and at great personal sacrifice . . . something is still missing.

The peace (or fellowship) offering focused on the worshiper's peace with God—the joy and peace of mind that come from knowing that God is at peace with us. This also spilled over to peace in the community, as the priests would receive most of this offering for their own sustenance. It was the only offering associated with a meal; the peace was shared by all.[4] This offering, and the fellowship it inspired (not just human to God, but person to person), was essentially a joyous celebration—a rejoicing community celebrating under the canopy of God's peace.[5]

Yet as much as there was feasting and celebration among the people, God was not at the party. Something kept Him away. Something is still missing.

As true as the worship was, and even though the choicest offerings were brought, there was one special ingredient that created the fragrance God longed to have permeate the worship brought before Him.

That ingredient was *justice.* If it was missing, all else was rejected.

> But let justice roll like water,
> and righteousness as a permanent torrent
> (Amos 5:24, *Postmodern Bible*).

Beneath the veneer of proper liturgy and awesome worship, something lurked in the community of God's people that ruined the whole experience for the One who should have been the center of it all. If worship truly is about the audience of One, then we must get this piece figured out or it's all for nothing—because He's simply not listening.

The poor were mistreated. There was injustice at all levels of civilization, from the marketplace to the judicial system. And God was not pleased. The element meant to set apart the worship of the Hebrews—the element that turned the burning flesh of animals, the offerings of grain and the melodies and rhythms of their music from just pagan acts of barbarism and fertility rites into worship that unlocked the gladness of heaven—was *justice demonstrated in community.* Jesus would call it "love."

As far removed as we are today from the sacrifice of lambs, goats and bulls, we are still called to the sacrifice of love demonstrated through justice. As complete as is the work of Christ on our behalf before the Father, obliterating the need for any and all blood sacrifice, we are called to a new commandment: to love one another.

As much as it was the element that set apart Jewish worship from the pagan rites of the nations around her, so too it is the vital element in our worship: that which sets us apart from the world around us is love expressed through justice. It is the mark of the Church, the identifying sign of all those who follow Jesus, for as He said: "The world will know that you are my disciples by your love for one another" (John 13:35).

Our worship should be a sweet perfume to the nostrils of God, and the secret ingredient for that aroma remains the same today as it was so long ago: *The fragrance of worship is justice . . . and where there is no justice, there is no fragrance.*

Notes

1. "The Grain or Meal Offering," Watton on the Web Christian Resource Center. http://www.watton.org/studies&stories/feasts/feasts2.htm (accessed March 21, 2006).

2. Bob Deffinbaugh, Th.M., "Leviticus: Sacrifice and Sanctification—The Grain Offering," Bible.org. http://www.bible.org/page.asp?page_id=260 (accessed March 21, 2006).

3. Ibid.

4. Ibid.

5. "Worship and Service: Fellowship," Eastside Christian Church (Fullerton, CA) online resource. http://www.becomingcloser.org/Worship/fellowship.htm (accessed March 21, 2006).

CHAPTER 3

ONE THING YOU LACK

"Mom," I whispered urgently, "Jesus says that
rich people don't go to heaven!"
"We are not rich. Go back to bed," came
my mother's response.

STACEY ELIZABETH SIMPSON[1]

I don't think I've ever been angrier.

I sat in my study (which was really just the spare bedroom), my Bible open to a passage in Galatians that had just struck me between the eyes. The truth that tilted my brain at that moment seemed so basic, so simple. Yet as I sat surrounded by row upon row of books, seminar notes, articles, manuals, video and audio cassettes, I couldn't remember any one of them clueing me in to what I had just read. Amid these words and words and words and words—literally tons of verbiage—had this never been mentioned or reflected upon? I'm sure it must have been, but never with enough intensity that it rattled me the way I was shaken that day. It seemed so important! How could I have missed this?

I could feel something burn deep inside and the sting of it has never left me.

I was mad.

I looked again:

All they asked was that we should continue to
remember the poor, the very thing I was eager
to do (Gal. 2:10).

The *One Thing*

Here we have a story that relates the very first intentional and strategic missional adventure in the history
of the Church. The gospel had spread through perse-
cution and the movements of people across the
Roman Empire, but until this moment no one had
been sent out in an intentional way to spread the news
of the Kingdom into cultures beyond the epicenter of
the Church in Jerusalem. Paul felt called to move out,
into potentially hostile Gentile territory. It was time,
and the key Church leaders agreed. The next phase in
the commission that Christ had given was about to
begin. History was being made.

To receive their blessing and instruction, Paul met
with these key figures: Peter, the Rock, the wild man
whose passion and spontaneity won him a place in the
inner circle of Christ's friends and propelled him into
a prominent role in the Early Church; James, the half-
brother of Jesus, nicknamed "Camel Knees" for the

huge calluses that had formed on his knees as he labored in prayer over the Church in Jerusalem, his flock; and John the Beloved, closest friend of Christ on Earth and a man of deep feeling and prophetic insight. These leaders had only one concern, one requirement for Paul as he sought to establish the Christian faith in unknown territory.

The stakes were mind-blowingly high. At this critical juncture for the followers of Jesus, they *had* to get this right. Of all the things they could have charged Paul to communicate, of all the things they felt was central to see Christian community established, they emphasized *one thing*. Of all the major concerns about the emerging articulation of theology that the Church was wrestling through, there was only *one thing* they knew must at all costs be practiced. If just this *one thing* was in place, everything else would sort itself out. If this *one thing* was observed, the gospel would be presented with integrity and the true faith would be demonstrated. Just one thing was required.

Remember the poor.

Sounds a little bit like Amos, right?

As is the case more often than not, scholars squabble about the whos and whats that appear in Scripture, and it's true here as well. They disagree whether this

call by the apostles to remembrance of the poor indi-
cates the impoverished saints in Jerusalem or is a reference to the poor everywhere, at all times.[2]

My conviction is that it's a combination of the
two. We know the Jerusalem apostles ministered
unceasingly to poor and hungry people in their midst.
The Church was overflowing with folks who did not
have enough to eat, and every day the apostles visited,
counseled and prayed with them. Because this ministry to the broken was so vital a part of the apostles'
daily ministry, it follows that they would have consid-
ered the poor of ultimate importance when the time
came to extend the gospel to other parts of the world.

The startling thing is that Paul seemed aston-
ished that the leadership would raise the question of
his concern for the poor. You can almost hear the surprise in his voice when he said, "That is the very thing
I was eager to do." Paul had been part of the Church
community for some time now—almost 20 years—
and the *one thing* that had captured his heart completely was ministry with the poor. What a statement
on the centrality of caring for the poor and marginalized in the heart of the Kingdom message!

I can't remember anyone *ever* saying that the
most exciting thing about being a part of the faith

community is its role with the poor. I've seen people clambering over each other to be a part of all kinds of programs and positions, but I have yet to see people scrapping over chances to be with the poor and complaining that there is no room for them to express their gifts in the "mercy department" of the Church.

Paul said it was the *one thing* he was most eager to do. What was it about Christian community and worship that had the needs of the poor and care for the oppressed so at the core of their identity that Paul would be so captivated? More important, what was it about Jesus Himself that so gripped the apostles that when they began to build community together after His ascension, this compassion was the hallmark of who they were and the *one thing* they wanted modeled as the Church began to move beyond Jerusalem?

Steve Zeisler, pastor of the Peninsula Bible Church in Palo Alto, California, has this to say about the *one thing*:

This aside illustrates clearly and beautifully what it means to be free in Christ, what it means to be Christian from the inside out rather than from the outside in. These men are saying they have a natural, inevitable, eager, undeniable concern for the needy, the poor, for those who do not have the material or emotional resources to make it in life. What a contrast with the approach taken by the legalists! Jesus chided the Pharisees who would tithe to the last seed in their garden, who would literally count out the seeds of their produce so that they got ten percent exactly to give to the work of God and to the poor but at the same time they did not care "about justice and the love of God." There are legalists today in the Christian cause who have a mechanical approach to being concerned for poor people. Their contribution to the United Way or some other charity is made automatically through a payroll deduction. Their conscience is thus dealt with and they can pat themselves on the back for it.

These people who met in Jerusalem knew poor people. They did not remember poverty, they remembered the poor. This was true of the pillars in Jerusalem and it was true in the eagerness of Paul's heart. Poor people—those whose material, emotional, and social resources were depleted—mattered to him. What a beautiful contrast with the mechanical, form-filling, long-distance, check-the-box approach we are familiar with today! These men lived with the needy and the overwhelmed. They prayed for them by name. They knew them because they were involved with them.[3]

Why hadn't anybody enlightened me about the *one thing*? I had a degree and multiple hours of teaching and instruction on everything from church mechanics to church growth to church planting to leadership development. Yet I can't remember anyone telling me the *one* requirement of the apostles.

That day in my study, the words of Jesus to the rich young ruler in Mark 10:21 began to haunt me as well: "one thing you lack." Jesus looked at this kid and loved him. He was moved by the young ruler's dedication to the Law and his desire to please God. This young guy had kept the commandments and had worshiped with what he thought was all his heart, yet Jesus said, "one thing you lack"—just *one thing*. If the young man could just get one piece to fall into place, the kingdom of heaven would be accessible and he would taste eternal life:

> Go, sell everything you have and give to the
> poor, and you will have treasure in heaven.
> Then come, follow me (v. 21).

The kid couldn't do it, because he "had great
wealth" (v. 22).

Could I?

I began to see a pattern emerging between the
prophet Amos (there he is again!), the invitation of
Christ, and the mission of the Early Church: this
one thing, the absence of which would mar all the
rest. It wasn't the *only* thing, but it was the *one*
thing that demanded to be at the heart of following
Christ and worshiping God. The secret ingredient.
The fragrance.

So I was mad. I was frustrated. Why hadn't anyone told me?

Learning to Live the *One Thing*

I knew the Lord was leading us into church planting again. The fragrance of worship revelation and
these words in Galatians became critical as we
began a seven-year journey to establish and release

a community in an inner-city neighborhood among the poorest of the poor.

Some of my closest mentors and advisors at the time tried to discourage us from starting with the poor. Maybe you could eventually reach out to the poor, but you can't *start* with them and invite them to be the core of the community! I disagreed, and I am so glad I did. It was far from easy, but I wouldn't have done it any other way. These words set our course and continue to affect us to this day. They have guided our ministry and community where we live and have compelled me to establish international relationships that allow me to experience community with the poor overseas and see firsthand the fallout of injustice in other parts of the world.

There is no true worship without community. There is no true community without embracing the poor and creating a safe space for the abused, marginalized and oppressed to find sanctuary and Kingdom justice.

The worshiping community cannot—and *must not*—divorce itself from identifying with the poor. The broken and marginalized have a central place in the identity of the Church. They must not be just some distant program to which we donate money.

Expressing our faith to the society around us without the poor and oppressed at the core of that expression is to present something skewed and twisted. Just as there is no sweet fragrance for God to enjoy without justice, the Christianity we model to the world has no sweetness and our representation of the Kingdom falls short if we fail to remember the poor.

The early apostles knew this and were adamant that the poor not be forgotten. For them, remembering the poor wasn't about establishing programs and events that would wipe out poverty and demand justice for the oppressed. No, it was about embracing people and demonstrating the Kingdom that brings good news to the poor. "They did not remember poverty, they remembered the poor." Could it be that the poor and marginalized might be accepted—without being "fixed" first—and allowed to be at the center of community life?

This point was driven home to me on one of my first trips into a third-world environment. I made my way up into northeast India to meet with a group of church leaders from across Nepal, India, Tibet and Bhutan. To this day, I have not witnessed physical poverty on the scale I saw then. Almost everyone gathered there had never eaten three meals in a day. Ever.

Their clothing was in tatters, and hygiene was a luxury many could not afford. The lone man who showed up in a fairly decent suit had purchased it at tremendous cost; his family had not eaten for two weeks to afford it. But he just *had* to have the suit, because "a man of God *must* have a suit—it is clearly wrong to dress otherwise." (Yuck! I wonder where he learned that? This imposition of Western Church culture is as much a form of injustice as anything else. God forgive us, we have so much to learn.) Many of these new friends had spent time in prison for their faith, and several would return home to find their dwelling places burned to the ground by angry Hindu sadhus and Buddhist monks.

My worldview shattered. I had fully entered the zone called *culture shock*!

It was difficult to feel that I had anything at all to say in the presence of such simple yet powerful faith. But as I sat and listened, my guard began to drop and all our insecurities and position posturing began to fall away. We could just *be* with one another, encouraging and strengthening each other for this journey of the Kingdom. It was truly awesome.

One afternoon as we all sat on the dirt floor sipping chai and swapping Kingdom tales, I felt the cra-

ziest thought buzzing around in the back of my mind.
I soon began to realize that this was more than just a
distraction; it was the Holy Spirit trying to get my
attention. But I was puzzled by what I was hearing.

"Tell them to not forget the poor," is what the
Lord said.

Unable to dismiss this as some mosquito-induced
delusion, I began to argue with God (in my mind, of
course). *How can I tell them to remember the poor? These
are the poor!* Yet the thought persisted, becoming much
more like a command every moment I delayed, and
I began to get that insistent feeling that to not speak
up would be disobedience.

"Tell them to remember the poor. These are leaders. These are church planters. Some of them are taking the Kingdom into unreached areas. Tell them!"

I felt awkward and uncomfortable, yet somehow
I became willing and vulnerable enough to take the risk.

In the flow of teaching, I brought things around
to the Galatians 2 passage. Through a translator,
I explained my discomfort with what I was about to
share and made it very clear that I felt I was in no position to understand the conditions under which they
lived. I said that I was not a professional missionary,
I was simply a follower of Jesus like them and that this

truth had really pierced me. It was the word of God. It was up to them to figure out how it applied in rural Nepal, in the jungles of India, in the mountains of Tibet, and in the back hills of Bhutan. I could not speak to those situations, but truth was truth and they must open themselves to hear how the Holy Spirit would relate it to their circumstances.

I remember saying, "Don't forget the poor." The translator followed suit in the Nepali tongue (the common language all through the Himalayan mountain region). And then, silence . . .

I felt so foolish.

Then, slowly, they began to cry. A few began to weep quite loudly, and I thought for sure I had offended them and blown it. I sheepishly asked the translator what was happening. He looked at me with puzzlement and said, "Can't you see?"

I wasn't sure what he meant. "See what?"

"Can't you see," he replied. "They're repenting."

"Repenting of what?" I couldn't believe what he was saying. "Repenting of *what*? These *are* the poor!"

He translated as the leaders began to share their testimonies. All of them knew people who were poorer than they were. The gospel had brought my pastor friends some measure of blessing; the Kingdom had given them dignity and a place of leadership and recognition. But as they began to take those blessings for granted, they had begun to distance themselves from others in the name of respectability and leadership, pulling away from the impoverished more and more. Certain theologies and approaches to Christian living had given them cause to see the poor as more of an indictment upon them than a central part of Christian community.

I was stunned. My paradigm had shifted yet again. This whole issue of the place of the poor and bringing the justice of the Kingdom was critical to understanding and demonstrating the gospel of Jesus Christ.

Oh God, let me never lack this *one thing*, this secret ingredient of Kingdom life and worship: Remember the poor.

Notes

1. Stacey Elizabeth Simpson, "Who Can Be Saved?" *The Christian Century* (September-October 2000), p. 951.

2. Dr. Thomas L. Constable, "Notes on Galatians" (2005 edition), *Sonic Light.* http://www.soniclight.com/constable/notes/pdf/galatians.pdf (accessed March 22, 2006).

3. Steve Zeisler, "Retaining the Truth of the Gospel," Peninsula Bible Church, December 18, 1983 (updated July 25, 2001). http://www.pbc.org/dp/zeisler/3921.html (accessed March 22, 2006).

KINGDOM JUSTICE: DOING IT GOD'S WAY

There is no virtue so truly great and godlike as justice.

JOSEPH ADDISON

His hook was going to hurt somebody someday. "One Wing" was one guy with whom I had a major love-hate relationship. Our friendship taught me more about life than any other friendship I had ever experienced. But, man . . . some days . . .

On a crazy afternoon long before I knew him, he lay on his back with an arm draped over the railroad track, high from sniffing glue. Predictably enough, a train came by and took off his arm. It was a clean slice, as if it had been done in the finest of butcher shops. That's how he got the hook that stood in for his missing hand, and his nickname: One Wing.

Today, he was blustering around our office, mad as anything at the white man who had hit him with a car. Being part of the street community as a First Nations (native Canadian) came with its share of prejudice, especially as a glue-sniffer (the very bottom of the heap), but I suspected that there was more to the story than the tale of purposeful racism One Wing was telling.

Waving a notice from an insurance company in the air, he proceeded to inform us that the oppression of the system was beating him down yet again. *He* had been the victim, the one hit by a car—and now the insurance company was after *him* to pay up. It was a conspiracy at the highest levels! As he continued to rant, some of our young social-activist zealots joined in the fray and decried the establishment and all its abuses. Underneath the bravado however, One Wing was scared. He wasn't sure what would happen to him if he didn't pay up.

Then I had a thought.

"Hey," I said. "Come over here."

I asked One Wing if he had been high on glue when he was struck by the car—maybe wandering into the street just a little—or if the maniacal white menace had purposely driven up onto the sidewalk to hunt him down, scoring another hit for the establishment. After much prodding and a few jokes, he admitted that he *might* have been just the teensiest bit high. In fact (if he was to be totally honest), One Wing hardly remembered anything about the incident.

"Okay," I said, "I'm pretty sure that this guy was just on his way to work or something. He maybe has a couple of kids at home, a wife—he's just trying to get through his day. He's not driving around looking for Natives to pick off with his car." I was waxing eloquent now. "There he is, just driving along, and then all of a sudden there's this guy flying off the front of his bumper out of nowhere, sliding up the hood, and *wham!* This big ol' hook cracks into his windshield and shatters it."

One Wing smiled as he began to realize how crazy it must have been for the white guy. "Now," I said, "this guy totally freaks out: He's not sure how much he's hurt you, since you stumbled off in a glue-induced daze, and his car is wrecked. All he's trying to do is fix his car so he can provide for his family."

I let that sink in and then asked, "Did he stop?"

"Yes," One Wing grudgingly admitted.

"Did he check to see if you were okay?"

"Yes."

"He wasn't after you, man," I suggested. "Give the guy a break. He had to fix his car through his insurance, and that's why they're contacting you." I then went a bit further. "In fact, you would really help this guy if you could give just a little money to the insurance company. It would help him fix his car, and I'm sure his family would really appreciate it." I was pouring it on a bit thick at this point, but the light began to dawn on One Wing.

"Hey," he said, getting excited now, "I could take 10 dollars a month out of my welfare check and put it toward the payment . . . would that work?" I assured him that I would check into it, impressed that he'd be willing to take such a step.

After some discussion with a very shocked representative at the insurance company (who had assumed it was a lost cause), we worked out an arrangement. She was obviously confused as to why I would be helping someone like glue-sniffing One Wing, and she asked me my reasons. We were able to talk about God's heart for justice, about the poor, and about people coming together in peace to see things change. By the end of our talk, she was moved and pleased to be part of the unfolding plan. (I'd have given anything to overhear her subsequent discussions with her coworkers as the presumed-closed file was reopened!)

The next day—a bit to my surprise—there was a crumpled envelope on my desk, with "$10.00" written in a shaky hand across the top. I choked up as I realized that One Wing had followed through. Amazing.

I walked out into the communal area outside our offices and noticed a bunch of people huddled in the corner. As I got closer, I almost burst into laughter when I saw One Wing surrounded by some others from the streets. "And yeah, you know . . ." he was saying, "this guy, he's got a wife and a couple of kids, just trying to make it . . . and I'm helping him fix his car!"

I'll always look to this incident as a snapshot of Kingdom justice. The end result was community and relationship over retribution or the demand for rights. Somehow under the rule and reign of God's kingdom, true justice comes—and with it, peace. As we lay down our agendas to submit to His, we see each other in a way that is impossible without His kingdom reign.

So, What *Is* Justice?

I Googled the word "justice" and discovered that there are as many interpretations and applications of this word as the day is long. It is critical then, as we are moved through hearts of true worship to explore what justice means for the followers of Jesus, that we anchor our motivations and perceptions of justice in God's perspective and character.

What I have discovered is that finding and expressing Kingdom justice is not about *human rights* but about *God's ways*. Kingdom justice is not about politics and law as much as worship and obedience. Justice: setting things right. Righteousness: aligning ourselves with the ways and heart of God. Love: the summation of who God is—God *is* Love—and the law by which Christ's followers live. It is here near His heart that true community can flourish.

I am the Lord who practices steadfast love, justice, and righteousness in the earth. For in these things I delight, declares the Lord (Jer. 9:24, *ESV*).

I the Lord love justice (Isa. 61:8, *ESV*).

Job was a man who caught the heart of God in matters of justice. He was described as one who was "blameless and upright, one who feared God and turned away from evil" (Job 1:1, *ESV*). God Himself stated that there was none like Job in all the earth (v. 8). He rose early in the morning to offer burnt sacrifices and worship (v. 5). (Hmm . . . remember the haunting words of the prophet Amos?) But when the smoke of the morning sacrifice was a distant smudge on the horizon, justice was the way Job lived:

I delivered the poor who cried for help, and the orphan who had no helper. . . . I put on righteousness, and it clothed me; my justice was like a robe and a turban. I was eyes to the blind and feet to the lame. I was a father to the needy, and I investigated the case which I did not know. I broke the jaws of the wicked and

snatched the prey from his teeth (Job 29:12,
14-17, *NASB*).

Job's was a righteousness worn like a cloak. A justice put on like a robe and turban. A way of living.
Justice is not something static or a tool used to keep
order. There is order and alignment in biblical justice, because it flows from the character and heart of
God Himself. It is not an activity as much as it is an
attribute and aspect of character to be developed.
A way of living. A way of *seeing*.

It is important to note that "concepts of justice
with righteousness, mercy and salvation are inter-
woven, creating an image of the dimensions of the
justice of God."[1] Scanning the Old Testament writ-
ings, we discover two Hebrew words that are translated "justice" and its synonym "righteousness": *sedeq*
and *mispat*. Paul Mercer helps us understand the difference between these two words:

> *Sedeq* is a dynamic, active word for justice. It
> reflects a creative generosity (distributive jus-
> tice) which we might call the "spirit of justice."
> It is never used to speak of punishment (ret-
> ributive justice). It deals with God's positive

action in creating and sustaining community, particularly on behalf of the marginal members (the poor). *Sedeq* is not just an action, but also refers to the kind of situation resulting when justice is exercised and so in Scripture there are links between *sedeq* and peace, salvation, faithfulness, kindness and compassion. Gerard Von Rad says *sedeq* describes "the highest value in life, that upon which all life rests when it is properly ordered."

Mispat represents a more static, legal expression of the dynamic *sedeq*. But it is more than strict legal justice, and includes a sense of good will, of equity and equitable distribution, particularly of the land. When used of God's intervention, the concept conveyed is similar to that of a Royal commission into an area of possible injustice. Solomon, when given the opportunity to ask anything of God, chooses "discernment in administering *mispat*" (1 Kings 3:9-14).[2]

The theme of justice is found not only in the Old Testament, but it is also a topic on nearly every page of the New Testament. In fact, justice marked the ministry of Jesus and all those who would follow after Him. Christ in the Gospels is the fleshed-out fulfillment of the messianic predictions of the prophets and poets of the Old Testament. Listen to Isaiah:

> Here is my servant, whom I uphold,
> my chosen one in whom I delight;
> I will put my Spirit on him
> and he will bring justice to the nations.
> He will not shout or cry out,
> or raise his voice in the streets.
> A bruised reed he will not break,
> and a smoldering wick he will not snuff out.
> In faithfulness he will bring forth justice;
> he will not falter or be discouraged
> till he establishes justice on earth.
> In his law the islands will put their hope
> (Isa. 42:1-4).

No one who had ever walked the earth was like Jesus. No one had ever lived out the realities of the just, messianic heart like Him. With the power of the Spirit as His constant source of strength, He moved to the fringes of society to touch the bruised reeds and to gently restore the smoldering wicks of the discarded and outcast. He moved to the edges of the religious world of the Jews and the dominating society of the Romans to bring hope, healing, life and justice. This is *one thing* He will not give up on until His everlasting kingdom is established, where all brokenness, oppression and injustice will be banished forever.

In Luke 4:18-19, Jesus declares His agenda clearly in Jubilee and justice terms: "The Spirit of the Lord is on me . . . to preach good news to the poor . . . to proclaim the year of the Lord's favor." In Matthew 6:33, Jesus calls His followers to seek the kingdom of God above all things and the righteousness (or *justice*) it administers: "But seek first his kingdom and his righteousness, and all these things will be given to you as well." In Luke 14:13, He rails against the Pharisees for neglecting justice and the love of God and instructs His disciples: "when you give a banquet, invite the poor, the crippled, the lame, the blind."

Remember that when Jesus was challenged by John the Baptist's disciples regarding the authenticity of His messianic mission and identity, He simply said, "Go and tell John what you hear and see: the blind receive their sight and the lame walk, lepers are cleansed and the deaf hear, and the dead are raised up, and the poor have good news preached to them"(Matt. 11:4-5, *ESV*). Christ's care for and healing of the sick and demonized were His answer to John's doubt, confirming the truth of His identity. Both the Jewish system of law and the pagan religions of the day saw the chronically ill as cursed—unclean—to be avoided and shunned. The beggar class was made up predominantly of the sick and deranged who had no other way to survive, with no other point of access to society. The coming of Jesus changed all that, overturning those systems with the justice of the Kingdom.

Far beyond evangelism crusades and statistics, Jesus' call to His followers to become fishers of men and workers in the harvest was a rallying cry to rescue the "harassed and helpless ones, wandering like sheep without a shepherd with no protection from the oppression and weight of religion, politics and the hedonism of the privileged classes . . . [this call] was an invitation to join Jesus in his struggle to transform the existing order of power and privilege and establish a new order."[3] A new order of Kingdom justice.

The Result of Justice

According to the Kingdom order of Jesus, the only worship that has any integrity is anchored by a lifestyle of justice. It is no wonder, then, that Jesus is found here—then *and* now—among the broken reeds and smoldering wicks. And it's no wonder that whatever is done to the least of these is done to Him (see Matt. 25:40).

> Love and Truth meet in the street,
> Right Living [justice] and Whole Living
> [peace] embrace and kiss!
> (Ps. 85:10, *THE MESSAGE*).

The result of Kingdom justice is wholeness. The result of Kingdom justice is peace.

The meaning of *shalom* is to be whole, uninjured and undivided, and it is used in a variety of ways in Scripture, from describing the quiet order of domestic life to expressing the most profound spiritual experience. Shalom is a harmonious, caring community with God at its center. To dwell in shalom is to enjoy living before God with one's community and oneself.

Standing in that common room with One Wing and his audience, I *saw* the wholeness and peace that justice brings. As God began to work His kingdom justice, a broken Native man took his first steps toward dignity and healing as he helped "the white guy fix his car," holding his head high as he "shared with those in need" (see Eph. 4:28); an insurance adjuster was moved when she saw the effort of a community to support a simple attempt to make recompense; a community celebrated together; and my relationship with One Wing took a dramatic leap forward as I saw hope and good news brought to the poor. Something broke through that day. Justice and peace kissed.

Notes

1. Richard Beaton, "Messiah and Justice: A Key to Matthew's Use of Isaiah 42:1-4," *Journal for the Study of the New Testament* (1999), vol. 75, pp. 5-23.

2. Paul Mercer, "Justice and Health in the Bible," *Luke's Journal* (2000), vol. 5(4), pp. 4-7. http://www.cmdfa.org.au/lukes/2000Mercer.html (accessed March 23, 2006).

3. Beaton, "Messiah and Justice, A Key to Matthew's Use of Isaiah 42:1-4," pp. 5-23.

CHAPTER 5

DRAWING FROM THE WELL OF MERCY

Mercy is above this sceptred sway,
It is enthroned in the hearts of kings,
It is an attribute to God himself;
And earthly power doth then show likest God's
When mercy seasons justice.

WILLIAM SHAKESPEARE,
THE MERCHANT OF VENICE

Mercy rests at the center of worship and justice. It is what marks both our vertical and horizontal expressions of devotion to Christ, and it is what motivates us in His Kingdom work.

> Therefore, I urge you, brothers, in view of God's mercy, to offer your bodies as living sacrifices, holy and pleasing to God—this is your spiritual act of worship (Rom. 12:1).

The view is good from this center. Without the sight that mercy gives, our understanding of worship and the justice lifestyle it demands will always be slightly askew. Worship and justice must be done "in view of God's mercy." You cannot *get* God without *getting* mercy. But getting mercy is tough.

Scandalized by Mercy

I slumped against the wall of a tiny hotel bathroom in Arnhem, Holland, dizzy in the aftermath of a scandalous thought that had cut across my mind and spirit. My lack of strength to stand was not physical; it was paralysis in my *being* that had left me breathless and disoriented.

I was in Holland for the celebration marking the fiftieth anniversary of the end of World War II. I had been adopted into a Dutch family in Canada, and given the intensity of the event and my adoptive family's personal and tragic World War II history, what had occurred to me was deeply troubling. That day in a Dutch hotel bathroom, I heard the Holy Spirit say, "If Hitler had turned to me for forgiveness, I would have freely pardoned him."

What? Did I hear that right? Have I lost my mind?

As I fumbled through the rest of my morning, I found myself turning back to the prophetic literature, particularly a passage from Isaiah. It was one of Jesus' favorites, and it was quickly becoming one of my own:

> Seek the LORD while he may be found;
> call on him while he is near.

Let the wicked forsake his way
and the evil man his thoughts.
Let him turn to the LORD,
and he will have mercy on him,
and to our God, for he will freely pardon.
"For my thoughts are not your thoughts,
neither are your ways my ways," declares the LORD.
"As the heavens are higher than the earth,
so are my ways higher than your ways
and my thoughts than your thoughts.
As the rain and the snow come down from heaven,
and do not return to it without watering the earth
and making it bud and flourish,
so that it yields seed for the sower and bread for
    the eater,
so is my word that goes out from my mouth:
It will not return to me empty,
but will accomplish what I desire
and achieve the purpose for which I sent it"
(Isa. 55:6-11).

The lynchpin that holds together justice and worship is *mercy*. There is no real understanding of worship without mercy at its core, and the justice of God cannot be understood without mercy as its center. If we seek to worship in the fragrance of justice, we must draw from the well of mercy.

The understanding of a God who freely pardons even the truly wicked is far beyond our ability to comprehend, yet it is the foundation of the in-breaking kingdom of heaven. All worship and service to God must be understood from this vantage point.

Jesus spins a tale of God's scandalous mercy in Matthew 18:23-35:

> Therefore, the kingdom of heaven is like a king who wanted to settle accounts with his servants. As he began the settlement, a man who owed him ten thousand talents was brought to him. Since he was not able to pay, the master ordered that he and his wife and his children and all that he had be sold to repay the debt.
>
> The servant fell on his knees before him. "Be patient with me," he begged, "and I will pay back everything." The servant's master took pity on him, canceled the debt and let him go.
>
> But when that servant went out, he found one of his fellow servants who owed him a

hundred denarii. He grabbed him and began to choke him. "Pay back what you owe me!" he demanded.

His fellow servant fell to his knees and begged him, "Be patient with me, and I will pay you back."

But he refused. Instead, he went off and had the man thrown into prison until he could pay the debt. When the other servants saw what had happened, they were greatly distressed and went and told their master everything that had happened.

Then the master called the servant in. "You wicked servant," he said, "I canceled all that debt of yours because you begged me to. Shouldn't you have had mercy on your fellow servant just as I had on you?" In anger his master turned him over to the jailers to be tortured, until he should pay back all he owed.

This is how my heavenly Father will treat each of you unless you forgive your brother from your heart.

In today's economy, the debt the wicked servant was forgiven would equal three *billion* dollars; the amount he was owed was five *thousand* dollars! In light of the eternal judgment God has forgiven us, our gratitude should far outweigh any injustice we might ever face here on Earth. This is hard to grasp, but it is an essential truth that we must wrestle through. In view of God's mercy, we abandon our agendas for His. We rest in His love, becoming living sacrifices who long for His appearance when all will be set right forever.

We must not demand our rights before seeking to understand the great mercy that God has extended to us as His adopted children. Forgiveness—the outworking of mercy—is the starting point of our relationship with God, and it must be the beginning of our human relationships as well.

The application of this truth becomes even more difficult when the injustice is almost beyond comprehension. Can the sexually abused find this forgiveness and freedom? Can an immigrant who has been taken advantage of by government policy and employers who cheat him or her out of a fair wage draw from the well of mercy? Can those who carry the deep wounds of racism and oppression rise up to bow down in a place of worship, anchored in mercy and forgiveness?

In this just and merciful Kingdom, there is hope for the oppressor as well as the oppressed. There is mercy for *all*, without concern for human standards of fairness. God's standard of justice reigns.

> I will show mercy to anyone I choose, and I will show compassion to anyone I choose (Rom. 9:15, *NLT*; see also Exod. 33:19).

As I sit in my North American home wrestling with these teachings of Christ and shifting my perspective outside my own comfortable world, I am ashamed at my pettiness when I realize there are countless thousands of His followers living out this hard mercy in the face of abuse and oppression unlike any I have ever experienced. What about young girls ravaged in the sex trade of Asia? What about those beaten and bruised in the modern slave trade? What about those who are dying of diseases like AIDS and tuberculosis as a result of war, famine and corruption? What does their worship look like after they have encountered the living, merciful God?

Mercy is truly a gift and it is offered in such a way that justice is not negated. Mercy "sea-

sons" justice as "salt" seasons meat and gives
it flavor. Mercy follows justice and perfects it.
To pardon the unrepentant is not mercy, but
license. C. S. Lewis, a contemporary Christian
author, wrote: "Mercy will flower only when it
grows in the crannies of the rock of Justice:
transplanted to the marshlands of mere
Humanitarianism, it becomes a man-eating
weed, all the more dangerous because it is still
called by the same name as the mountain
variety."[1]

To worship here—to worship *this way*—demands a
deep humility. Justice must be initiated and sustained
by God's mercy and administered under His sover-
eignty. As the old hymn says: "trust and obey, for
there's no other way to be happy in Jesus."[2] All our
worship must flow from simple trust and with the
assurance that God has the ultimate perspective on
all things; that vengeance is His and His alone; and
that only He can rule. We lay down our crowns, we lay
down our lives, we lay down our rights, and—even as
we fight for justice—we know the ultimate Day of the
Lord will come. Then, in the light of a new heaven
and a new earth, justice will truly reign.

He will wipe every tear from their eyes. There
will be no more death or mourning or crying
or pain, for the old order of things has passed
away (Rev. 21:4).

Doing Justice, Loving Mercy

Some years after meeting Betty in the string of rundown
motels by my house, I met Charles. Early one morning,
I was walking through the entrance of our newly
acquired ministry center in the heart of Winnipeg. Once
upon a time it had been a bank, but after suffering one
too many robberies, the bigwig bankers had run for the
suburbs, leaving us with the building.

Bodies lay strewn across the floor of the enclosed
entryway. A good ol' Canadian prairie winter was set-
tling in, and this little hovel—formerly the ATM—was
one of the only warm places in this part of the city.
Passed out from cold and fatigue (and a bit too much
of the cheap alcohol they had hidden in the ceiling
tiles), the sleeping horde made it quite a challenge to
pick my way through to the front door of the office.
The smell (I told you it always gets me) was abrasive,
and I tried to hurry.

But then I stopped. Just in front of the door was a
man lying very still. Too still. Something nudged me

on the inside, and I *knew* something was wrong. The nudge was so strong that I forgot everything else and began to try to wake him from his drunken slumber. By this time, several other people began to awaken, quite frustrated by the ruckus I was making.

The man didn't move.

I continued to try to shake him awake, but nothing happened. So I did the only thing I could think to do. I stood up—and kicked him. This got quite a response from the onlookers; I'm sure they thought I was some white dude trying to pick a fight with the Native crowd. I assured them that I was there to help. And then kicked him again.

Finally, he began to stir . . .

That morning began a domino-series of events that would take me into a world I never knew existed. Through this one man—Charles—I gained entry into the community of poor in our city. Over the next years, Charles would have me laughing, crying, cursing, celebrating. He would take me through every possible emotion as I tried to hang on to our friendship. He became another mentor in my journey to see worship and justice kiss.

Without knowing what I was doing, I saved Charles's life that morning. Doctors told us later that if he hadn't been brought to consciousness, he would have drifted into a deep sleep from which he would never have awakened. But Charles did wake up, and then he taught me about mercy.

The truth is, Charles was one of the first people to give me a glimpse of mercy beyond easing my own conscience and feeling good about my self-sacrifice. Just *knowing* Charles helped me to understand what it was to love mercy. As I reflect back, I think he had to extend mercy to me more than I to him. There were pockets of prejudice and judgment inside me that I never knew existed; there were attitudes and stereotypes that had to be dismantled as I learned to be a friend to Charles, as we stumbled together along the path to discover what it means to follow Jesus in the brokenness of life.

His life was an incredible gift to me, because his struggle—lived out in the open, with no money, possessions or power to hide it—was an everyday reminder of the struggle we *all* face: how to be a broken human being in a sick and fallen world. Oftentimes, the only difference between the poor and the rich is that the poor have no resources with which to cover their flaws, sins and addictions. There is much to learn from this brutal honesty. May we never flinch in the face of such a gift.

Though Charles was never completely free from the claws of the glue addiction that shattered his life, and though he didn't quite "clean up" as we hoped, he knew Jesus. Eventually, street living and substance abuse took their inevitable toll, and despite our prayers and tears, Charles died. But he did not die without hope. He did not die without faith.

The two things Charles loved to do most were to laugh and sing, and shortly before he died he wrote a song—a worship song. In a strange twist of events, we recorded it (not knowing that he was going to die) and were able to play it at his funeral. Here is Charles's song:

> We should never say goodbye
> To all the things we try
> Follow the ways of Jesus Christ our Lord
> Because He died for our sins
> There's a place we can call home
> Follow the ways of Jesus Christ our Lord
>
> Follow the way
> Follow the truth
> Follow the life

Follow the way of Jesus Christ our Lord

Oh how I love to sing and worship Him
In the twilight of the night
Because anytime is alright by me
And we'll be with Jesus for eternity
Do not make pride your necklace
Remember grace, oh Lord
Follow the way of Jesus Christ our Lord

Take my hand, dear friend
Take off your shame
We'll be with Jesus Christ one day
Follow the ways of Jesus Christ[3]

Charles got it; he understood an aspect of faith that I still struggle to grasp. James called the poor "the chosen ones," those chosen to be rich in faith (see Jas. 2:5). They live and die knowing that mercy is their only hope. Oh God, grant me such sight, such wisdom.

I'll never forget the first time Charles sang his song for me. The smell of glue was strong in the air, yet the fragrance of heaven was so much stronger. His voice warbled just slightly off pitch, yet its timbre was so haunting and real that it captivated me. I wept. I wept when I heard it the first time, and I wept again when I heard Charles singing it from the grave, the CD piped through the funeral home's little sound system.

Mercy. To step away from a mercy-centered viewpoint will cause our worship and the justice lifestyle that flows from it to skew.

> With what shall I come before the LORD
> and bow down before the exalted God?
> Shall I come before him with burnt offerings,
> with calves a year old?
> Will the LORD be pleased with thousands of rams,
> with ten thousand rivers of oil?
> Shall I offer my firstborn for my transgression,
> the fruit of my body for the sin of my soul?
> (Mic. 6:6-7).

Who is this God? How must I serve Him? The answer:

> He has showed you, O man, what is good.
> And what does the LORD require of you?
> To act justly and to love mercy
> and to walk humbly with your God (Mic. 6:8).

Steeped in humility, we are called to act justly and to love mercy. Don't miss this! Justice is an *action*, to be done in and through the power of Christian community, *but mercy is to be loved*. It is not an action; it is a passion.

It is hard to love mercy. My first attempts at "mercy ministry" were quite pathetic: They were more self-serving than I could admit. My motivations were an eased conscience, a sense of self-sacrifice, and an awareness of how *good* I was—not justice for the people I was trying to serve. Mercy was not about touch, closeness and friendship; it was about works, to help my standing before God. I could *do* mercy and remain unchanged. But to *love* mercy . . . that's a different thing altogether.

Mercy is tricky. It levels the playing field. It demands that I draw near, to touch and engage. It is mercy that keeps me humble and able to keep step with God. As Shakespeare noted, mercy "seasons" justice and is the mark that distinguishes God's justice from that which is merely human—a justice infinitely higher than our thoughts and ways. We must draw from this well of mercy if we are ever to worship in the fragrance of justice.

Notes

1. Don Schwager, "The Unforgiving Official or The Unmerciful Servant," RCNet. http://www.rc.net/wcc/parabl42.htm (accessed March 25, 2006).

2. John Hammis, "Trust and Obey," (1887), music by Daniel B. Towner. Online version at *The Cyber Hymnal.* http://www.cyberhymnal.org/htm/t/r/trstobey.htm (accessed March 25, 2006).

3. Charles Moar, "Follow," *No Fixed Address,* Howling Prairie Music, © 2001. Used by permission.

CHAPTER 6

BEYOND THE PROGRAM:
The Way of Kingdom Love—Friendship

> Let us more and more insist on raising funds of love,
> of kindness, of understanding, of peace. Money will
> come if we seek first the Kingdom of God.
>
> MOTHER TERESA

In 1994, a Pulitzer Prize-winning photograph was taken during the Sudan famine that shocked the world. The picture shows a famine-stricken child in the foreground crawling toward a United Nations food camp, a long kilometer away for a starving child. In the background, a vulture crouches, watching . . . waiting for the child to die so it can eat him.

Economist and author Thomas Sowell estimates that nearly 70 cents for every dollar intended for a needy beneficiary gets burned up in bureaucratic transfer costs.[2]

No one knows what happened to the child, including the photographer, Kevin Carter, who left the Sudan just after the photo was taken.

Three months after he snapped the picture, Kevin committed suicide.[1]

This tragedy is a powerful example of what the journey into justice will be without friendship at the heart of the adventure. It will be difficult to know who we are feeding: the "vultures" or those truly in need.

The poor are big business. There is money to be made in the name of charity.

In the labyrinth of grants, foundations, NGOs and fund-raisers, a lot of cash flows through a lot of fingers.

A sagging music career or a TV star in need of a little PR boost can get a lot of mileage out of a photo op with the less fortunate.

Charity can grab some awesome tax breaks, at least in North America. There are great incentives in the tax system, and generosity can reap great financial benefits.

Addressing social injustice can win votes at the ballot box. Timing is critical (and you certainly want to leave yourself an out), but a lot of points can be won in the public arena by posturing on the right issues.

And giving money to the homeless or supporting a program in the church or on TV is an excellent way to sow "faith seed"—to get that kickback from heaven and a download of prosperity (all for the Kingdom, of course).

The Approach of Jesus
"If I give all I possess to the poor and surrender my body to the flames, but have not love, I gain nothing"

(1 Cor. 13:3). The root of injustice is the abuse of power and resources. It is the absence of selfless love. To approach doing justice by thinking the answer is power and resource in the right hands (ours) is to risk becoming a perpetrator of injustice.

Jesus' approach refuses to risk it. This great Advocate of justice, come to free the world from all forms of spiritual and physical injustice, slavery and abuse, chose a route other than power. In fact, He *concealed* His power. He refused to use His position of messianic authority to accomplish His Kingdom destiny. He humbled Himself, becoming one of those He came to save.

> Think of yourselves the way Christ Jesus thought of himself. He had equal status with God but didn't think so much of himself that he had to cling to the advantages of that status no matter what. Not at all. When the time came, he set aside the privileges of deity and took on the status of a slave, became *human*! Having become human, he stayed human. It was an incredibly humbling process. He didn't claim special privileges. Instead, he lived a selfless, obedient life and then died a

selfless, obedient death—and the worst kind of death at that: a crucifixion (Phil. 2:5-8, *THE MESSAGE*).

In reflecting on this passage, John Calvin wrote:

> In order to exhort us to submission by His example, He shows that when as God He might have displayed to the world the brightness of His glory, He gave up His right, and voluntarily emptied Himself; He assumed the form of a servant, and, contented with that humble condition, suffered His divinity to be concealed under a veil of flesh.[3]

In true meekness and gentleness of heart, Jesus holds back His power. This great King advances His Kingdom through the love of mercy and a humble heart of justice. Instead of the frontal assault we might attempt (and even enjoy), He brings the Kingdom through the back door, producing change as yeast in a loaf or the slow stealth of a mustard seed. He goes against all reason by allowing tares and wheat to grow together. His approach doesn't seem impressive—or even effective—at first glance, but in the great light of eternity, true change and freedom is wrought as His kingdom is established under the banner of love.

This is far from a heavenly handout or a program from on high to get "fixed." This is not salvation at a distance. This is *Emmanuel*, God with us—mercy incarnate and justice from the grass roots, demonstrated through the simplicity of love and friendship.

Christ gives an invitation in Matthew 11:28-30; an invitation to come to Him and be free from all bondage and oppression, an invitation to walk into relationship with Him:

> Come unto me, all ye that labour and are heavy laden, and I will give you rest. Take my yoke upon you, and learn of me; for I am meek and lowly in heart: and ye shall find rest unto your souls. For my yoke is easy, and my burden is light (*KJV*).

This is how Jesus approaches humanity: In moving toward our brokenness, coming as the One who will not crush the bruised reed or extinguish the smoldering wick, He comes as one who is *meek*.

The meaning of the word translated "meek" in this passage, *prautes*, is difficult to express in English.

The English word "meek" suggests weakness or frailty, but prautes suggests nothing of the kind. We need to understand that the meekness of Jesus is the fruit of power, power that comes with having the infinite resources of God at His command. Jesus also gives this power to reject self-concern to those who follow Him. In knowing God is on our side, we can be meek as Jesus was meek.[4]

The Currency of Jesus

When Jesus sent His disciples out to advance the work of the Kingdom, He gave this funny piece of advice: "Don't take any money with you" (Matt. 10:9, *NLT*). It's no wonder that Peter later responded to a lame beggar's request for cash by saying, "I don't have any money for you. But I'll give you what I have. In the name of Jesus Christ of Nazareth, get up and walk!" (Acts 3:6, *NLT*).

Don't get me wrong; money and resources definitely have a role in redressing injustice, and at times, justice can be administered through the halls of political power; the Christian community must have a voice there. But money and power can create the temptation to exchange love and justice for *charity*. In Kingdom currency, that is never a good exchange. Instead of charity, we must seek *friendship*.

Our worship should bring us to a point of encounter: an encounter with God and an encounter with our neighbor. Sometimes money and resources (or lack thereof) can get in the way of people encountering one another, even in the pursuit of justice. To lose this point of encounter is to lose the power of the exchange. For when we touch the poor and oppressed, an exchange—a miracle—takes place: *We are changed* in the encounter. Far beyond rich helping poor, strong helping weak, privileged reaching down to underprivileged, or (perhaps the worst of all) "holy" touching "sinner," this is an exchange of life and love. Friendship.

An old mentor of mine used to say it this way: "This whole journey is just about one beggar helping another beggar find out where the bread is." Where it really matters, we are all the same. We are all in need of God. We are all in need of mercy. We are all equal at the foot of the Cross.

Our desire is not that others might be relieved while you are hard pressed, but that there might be equality. At the present time your plenty will supply what they need, so that in turn their plenty will supply what you need. Then there will be equality, as it is written: "He who gathered much did not have too much, and he who gathered little did not have too little" (2 Cor. 8:13-15).

Friendship demands *equality*, which is not some communistic ideal or socialist philosophy, but the level ground in the realm of the Kingdom. The mountains are brought low, the valleys are raised up, the crooked places made plain. There is level ground at the foot of the Cross.

Bono, activist and lead singer of the group U2, spoke earnestly about the necessity of equality at the National Prayer Breakfast in February 2006:

Here's the bad news. From charity to justice, the good news is yet to come. There is much more to do. There's a gigantic chasm between the scale of the emergency and the scale of the response. And finally, it's not about charity after all, is it? It's about justice.

Let me repeat that: It's not about charity, it's about justice.

And that's too bad.

Because you're good at charity. Americans, like the Irish, are good at it. We like to give, and we give a lot, even those who can't afford it. But justice is a higher standard. Africa makes a fool of our idea of justice; it makes a farce of our idea of equality. It mocks our pieties, it doubts our concern, it questions our commitment.

Sixty-five hundred Africans are still dying every day of a preventable, treatable disease, for lack of drugs we can buy at any drug store. This is not about charity, this is about justice and equality.

Because there's no way we can look at what's happening in Africa and, if we're honest, conclude that deep down, we really accept that Africans are equal to us. Anywhere else in the world, we wouldn't accept it. Look at what happened in South East Asia with the tsunami. 150,000 lives lost to that misnomer of all misnomers, "mother nature." In Africa, 150,000 lives are lost every month. A tsunami every month. And it's a completely avoidable catastrophe.

It's annoying, but justice and equality are mates, aren't they? Justice always wants to hang out with equality. And equality is a *real pain.*[5]

Friendship: The Great Exchange

When we began to establish a new community among the urban poor, the needs seemed so overwhelming and our abilities and resources so limited that we didn't know where to begin other than on our faces before God. So we started with a regular rhythm of worship and intercession. Almost daily, we huddled in our little ministry center, cranking up the sound system and pouring our hearts out to God. Intercession was sweet, and the more we made friends among the poor in our city, the more passionate our cry became on their behalf.

I'm not sure exactly when things shifted, but one day I remember looking up and noticing that there were a handful of people from among the working poor, the welfare class and the street community hanging out in the back of the room. They'd pulled up some chairs, somehow feeling comfortable just being with us as we sang and prayed. I nodded and smiled, not thinking much of it.

But over time, more and more people came. For some reason, they showed up especially on Tuesday mornings. Now you must understand: In the beginning, we didn't serve soup or sandwiches and had no mechanism for clothing distribution. There was a coffee urn at the back, bubbling up some of the worst coffee in the city, but beyond that . . . nothing. Yet they continued to come.

We were amazed when we realized that *they just wanted to be with us.* With religious posturing stripped from our gathering and a sincere heart-cry bleeding through our music and inter-cession, they felt safe and found that they could identi-fy with our brokenness before God. They liked that. More than another soup line or shelter, they liked it here on level ground.

> There is always the danger that we may just do the work for the sake of the work. This is where the respect and the love and the devotion come in—that we do it to God, to Christ, and that's why we try to do it as beautifully as possible.
>
> —Mother Teresa

There should be no place on Earth where the ground is more level than in the place of worship. It is here at the foot of the Cross where worship and justice kiss. Here, when a cup of cold water is given to the "least," it is given to Christ Himself. This is worship.

Friendship: The Beginning of Community

The place was a bit of a dive, but we loved the food. It was right across from our ministry center, so the loca-tion was handy, too. Some friends had just left, and my good friend Jan and I were sitting on the same side of the booth, chatting it up, nursing our coffee just a little longer.

Someone plunked down across from us. Startled, we looked over to see someone from the streets whom we had never laid eyes on before (and never did again, frankly). He was a bit snarly—and a lot tipsy.

"We've been watching you," he blurted out. "We've been watching you for quite some time now. And you know what? We're starting to believe that you actually *like* us. Lots of programs down here, lots of ways to get food and some clothes . . . you need your religious system, and we know how to work it. But something's different about you guys . . . we think you actually *care* about *us*."

Jan and I sat there with our mouths hanging open.

"You're good soldiers," he continued. "You're good soldiers. Keep it up."

Then he got up and walked out of the restaurant, leaving our eyes glistening with tears and our hearts challenged.

We'd been hanging in the inner city for about three years, knowing that it would take time to build trust and establish relationships beyond programs and strategies. Thank God, something was finally shifting. Soon after our strange restaurant encounter, our community began to evolve into something beyond a church with programs, schedules and meetings. (I remember someone praying for us once, without knowing who we were or what we were up to in the inner city. That person asked the Lord to "bless their parish." That's really what we were becoming.) Marriages, funerals—way too many, but an urban reality—and celebrations became a part of who we were. We were truly becoming a *community* center.

From the level of the street subculture to the places of municipal government, people were sent our way because we were the place that *really cared* for people. Social Services called us up to refer people and asked for our input. One of our city council members even took an interest in what we were doing and made contact. Our reputation began to spread because we were known for relationship first, not programs. The power of friendship spoke louder than systems and structures.

We had exchanged charity for friendship.

Friendship: Laying Down Your Life

"Greater love has no one than this, that he lay down his life for his friends" (John 15:13). The layers of Jesus' meaning are elusive at first glance. How can laying down my life for a *friend* be the greatest form of love? Maybe my enemy—that sounds more like it. Maybe giving it all up for the down and out, for the beneficiaries of my great kindness and spiritual sacrifice. That's more like it. But a *friend*?

Jesus was known as a friend of sinners (see Matt. 11:19), and it was much more than a nickname for a guy on a mission of mercy. It was far beyond an act of sacrifice on behalf of the human condition. Jesus stepped close, close enough to call us *friends*.

And it got Him into trouble.

Now the tax collectors and "sinners" were all gathering around to hear him. But the Pharisees and the teachers of the law muttered, "This man welcomes sinners and eats with them" (Luke 15:1-2).

The Son of Man came eating and drinking, and you say, "Here is a glutton and a drunkard, a friend of tax collectors and 'sinners'" (Luke 7:34).

Jesus' involvement with sinners was so up-front and close that He was seen as a friend. There was no mistaking His actions as those of a teacher imparting

morals or a leader trying to help His hapless followers. He was a friend. The religious leaders could not
understand His ridiculous posture of friendship!

To follow Christ is to be drawn past the activities
and programs of justice and into friendship. This
takes us beyond the *obligation* of a life of worship to a
place of true selflessness, and in this place, love is
unlocked. No greater love exists than that of a selfless friend.

Could I die for my enemy?

Would I die for those on the margins of society?

Maybe.

But the *real* question is, Can I allow myself to
step over the seen and unseen lines that separate
races, tribes, classes, economic conditions, educa-
tional accomplishments and languages and move
with a heart of friendship? Not to fix people or save
them . . . not as an outreach or a program . . . but
as a friend?

Remember One Wing, the one-armed, glue-sniffing guy who helped "the white man fix his car"? One
day, I was walking to one of our community gatherings. A couple blocks ahead was a gang house, and as
I drew near, several dangerous-looking young men
came out onto the porch, their attention drawn to

something coming around the adjoining street corner.

As I got closer, I saw it wasn't something . . . it was *someone*.

"Hey, sniffer!" they called out. (As I mentioned, glue addicts are the bottom of the heap in street hierarchy, and the gangs love to torment them.)

I couldn't believe my eyes. It was One Wing, sauntering down the sidewalk.

"Hey, sniffer . . . get over here!"

This was not good. I could see the fear in One Wing's eyes, but this was not a situation that I wanted to be in the middle of. These gang bangers were not the kind of guys you messed with and came out fine and dandy. *Oh, man . . . what am I going to do?* I thought. I had a horrible feeling that I had just entered the Friend Zone, and that this whole setup was more about me and Jesus than anyone else. *Greater love has no one than this . . .*

My stomach tied itself in knots, but before I could talk myself out of it, I said—no, yelled, "HEY!"

Everything went into slow-motion—you know, like those really terrifying dreams where everything slows down and you try to run but nothing seems to move fast enough and there is absolutely no chance that you will escape alive or at least with all your limbs intact. The whole world slowed down as the gang guys turned in my direction, wanting to see who would be fool enough to stick his nose into this situation.

As I think back on that moment of my life, the next words spoken *at* me still leave me breathless. About as far from gang lingo as you can get, it was as if some demon was issuing a challenge.

"What do you have to do with him?" one of the bangers screamed.

I heard myself say, "He's my friend."

With what I believe was the help of the Holy Spirit, I spoke out a truth that changed me. The impact of those words hit me far harder than it did the gang guys (or One Wing, for that matter—he saw his opportunity for escape in the brief distraction I created, and before I even finished the sentence he was hoofing it down the street, around a corner and out of sight). As I spoke, I realized something: On that moment, *One Wing had become my friend*—and that changed everything. I can honestly say that I would have laid down my life for him. I will never read John 15:13 the same again.

Jesus came *as a friend*. He chose to call us friends, and His liberating love flows from that place. If we are to touch the liberating power of justice and have it be more than activism, politics, programs and self-serving activities that are more about easing our consciences than engaging with real people, we must have the courage to become friends.

Story Time: Where There Is No Friendship

His name was Southside Johnny, and he was an enigma of a man. He had one of the most brilliant minds I have ever encountered. Give him any subject—and I mean *any* subject—and he could wax eloquent for hours. He knew sports, politics, music, architecture, law . . . you name it, he knew it.

Johnny was also incontinent and one of the meanest guys you'd ever want to meet when he was drunk—which made it hard to get to know him, since he was drunk a lot of the time. But slowly, I did. It took some time, but he began to trust.

After I had known him a while, one of the local news stations did a full-on story of Southside Johnny's life. It turns out that he had been one of the wealthiest men in the city. Long before I arrived, he was a major wheeler-dealer in the real estate business. He made a fortune, but then the bottom dropped out. Johnny lost everything, money included. In the middle of his downslide, he came home to find his wife in bed with another man, and a few weeks later he was diagnosed with leukemia. Now, Johnny was on the skids.

The reporter told the whole sordid story. Ripples of excitement began to spread through the various programs and services that littered the inner city. Before the news feature, Johnny had tried to tell people his story, but no one would listen. They thought it was all just tall tales made up by some crazy street bum. But now, everybody wanted a piece of him. Johnny had all kinds of people chasing him to become one of their ministry or program or charity success stories. It was sickening, especially from Johnny's point of view.

Shortly after his story aired on television, Johnny burst into one of our Sunday gatherings. Yelling at the top of his lungs, smelling of pee and cheap alcohol, he cried, "I love you guys!"

All heads turned to see him stumbling up the center aisle.

"You guys liked me even when you didn't know my story. I told all those other people to f— off! You guys are the real deal . . . you want *me*. This is where I'm staying."

I sat with a dear friend in a church building that had multiple flags hanging high on the walls. The flags represented all the nations where the church had sent people and resources. It was quite impressive. Their efforts had gone toward establishing orphanages and social services in many parts of the world.

My friend was from one of those places. Although he was grateful for all the resources generated by this church, he still ached. There was very little relational connection, let alone any sense of true friendship.

"I'll take their money," he said. "I'll take it and make sure it gets to those who need it." His eyes welled up with tears. "But for me . . . all I am to them is just another flag on the wall."

I've already told you about my first trip to northeast India, a life-changing time to say the least. Each evening, we ministry leaders gathered together and shared a communal meal. It was very simple, but the rice was good quality and every night there was some kind of meat mixed in with the *dal*—a very special treat for many who had hardly ever eaten meat in their lives. (Another aspect of the meal—and a challenge for me— was no utensils: We ate with our hands, which was especially tricky since there was no toilet paper to use while visiting the famous Asian "squatty-potties.")

As we chowed-down on one such meal, I noticed several people staring at me. They looked quite upset. I wasn't sure what was wrong, so I asked a few questions and discovered that they were far from upset: They were moved.

"The 'preacher man' never eats *with* us," they said. "He always goes to the hotel to sleep and eat . . . Why are you eating *with* us?"

Later on that same trip, I ended up in the city of Katmandu, a place I have come to love deeply. I made fast friends with a young couple who were followers of Jesus. As the only believer from his village in Nepal, the well-educated husband of this duo was in high demand by mission groups and agencies that were setting up shop in Nepal. He had many opportunities ahead of him.

The couple suggested that they assist me in finding a hotel for the night. My response was that I would much rather stay with them. I wanted to get to know them and to see Katmandu from their perspective, rather than from some isolated westernized hotel. They wrestled a bit, but eventually I ended up in their home.

It was a crazy night. The squatty-potty, the freezing night air, sleeping on the floor, the rat that stole my glasses while I slept and chewed off the nosepiece—it was quite an adventure. But I wouldn't have traded it for anything.

In the morning as we ate a simple breakfast together, the couple began to weep. "Thank you so much for coming," they said. "No Westerner has ever come to our home. The missionaries always meet us at the hotel restaurant or someplace else in the city. No one ever comes where *we* live. Thank you so much."

They were waiting by the window, watching for our arrival. As we pulled up to the condemned building where they lived, I couldn't believe that this little family found any kind of quiet here—let alone any peace.

Earlier I had found Randy, inebriated and beaten up. I'd never met him before, but something nudged me to come alongside and see what I could do to help him. It was obvious that I couldn't do much initially, but the spark of relationship was present and I was aware that this was a Holy Spirit setup that was as much about my journey as it was about what I might do for this broken First Nations man and his family. I didn't really know what to do, or what to say—but I heard myself tell him that I would come by later if he let me know where he lived.

So he told me.

They were waiting by the window. As a couple of friends and I went to the beat-up front door of the dilapidated building, Randy and Hazel and Donovan came running down the stairs to meet us. "No one ever comes," they cried. "No one *ever* actually comes. They all say they will, but they never do. Come on in . . ."

Some time later, I realized I hadn't been by to see Hazel in a while. I guess I just got busy. Randy had died not long ago when his brain finally fried as a result of all the substance abuse he'd put it through. It was tragic, but Jesus had him, and that was a comfort.

I was trying to leave my house (to go to church, ironically), when the phone rang. It was Hazel, and she was drunk.

"Why don't you come to see me anymore . . . where have you been?" she moaned with a slur. "You know why I ask for food? You know why? Do you think it's the food I want?"

She was yelling now. "Do you think it's the food? No! But that's the only way I can get you to come by. *I want to see you.*"

Now I'm in Los Angeles, meeting John and his "live-in," Tommy. From under the overpass bridge, I point up to one of the largest charity centers in the whole of the United States.

> We think sometimes that poverty is only being hungry, naked and homeless. The poverty of being unwanted, unloved and uncared for is the greatest poverty.
>
> —Mother Teresa

"Why don't you go up there?" I ask.

"Tried it," John says. "Program wasn't too bad . . . better than most. But they don't *know* me . . . not even sure if they know my name."

Here we go again . . .

Notes

1. "Photographer Haunted by the Horror of His Work," *Sydney Morning Herald,* July 30, 1994. Online version from "The Ultimate in Unfair," Flat Rock. http://www.flatrock.org.nz/topics/odds_and_oddities/ultimate_in_unfair.htm (accessed March 25, 2006).

2. Larry Elder, "The Space Libertine Choice," FrontPageMagazine.com, November 3, 2000. http://www.frontpagemag.com/Articles/Read Article.asp? ID=2701 (accessed March 25, 2006).

3. John Calvin, *Institutes of the Christian Religion*, Book 2, Chapter 13. Online version at the Ethereal Library. http://www.ccel.org/ccel/calvin/institutes.iv.ii.xiv.html?highlight=christ,clothed,true,substance, human, nature#highlight (accessed March 25, 2006).

4. Adapted from *Vine's Expository Dictionary of New Testament Words*, s.v. "meek," "meekness." http://www.menfak.no/bibelprog/vines.pl?word=meekness (accessed March 25, 2006).

5. Bono, "Bono's Remarks to the National Prayer Breakfast," speech given February 2, 2006, at the National Prayer Breakfast in Washington, D.C., DATA.org. http://www.data.org/archives/000774.php (accessed March 26, 2006).

CHAPTER 7

THE JOURNEY FROM HERE

Congregations committed to breaking from the status quo are called to develop a sense of "radical hospitality." Rather than seeking out like members for mutual support, they seek people who consider themselves beyond the reach of organized religion . . . Rather than limiting their public theology to outreach or charity that maintains the unjust distribution of power and resources, congregations formed in radical hospitality exercise a commitment to justice. This model seeks to transform both the believer and society as a whole.

SHERYL A. KUJAWA-HOLBROOK[1]

I arrive at the final portion of this manuscript feeling somewhat frustrated. I have not addressed the larger scope of justice theology and practice that can move us to tackle the big issues such as abortion, AIDS, the sex-slave trade, illegal immigration, corrupt government, and abuse in the judicial system. But if we begin with the simple steps of worship, mercy and friendship, we will eventually be led to tackle the big-ticket concerns. And the truth is, the principles that guide us in the little things are the same that will guide us as we strike at the larger issues of poverty and injustice in our world.

Just as the Messiah "will not falter or be discouraged till he establishes justice in the earth" (Isa. 42:4), we as His followers cannot but be caught up in the wake of His righteousness and justice. The passion to see things set right under the dominion and order of God's kingdom should burn in all of us, and the highest calling of those who worship in this domain is to go to the lowest places with the hope and healing the gospel always brings.

The fragrance of worship is justice . . . where there is no justice, there is no fragrance.

Go and Learn

"While Jesus was having dinner at Matthew's house, many tax collectors and 'sinners' came and ate with him and his disciples. When the Pharisees saw this, they asked his disciples, 'Why does your teacher eat with tax collectors and "sinners"?' On hearing this, Jesus said, 'It is not the healthy who need a doctor, but the sick. But go and learn what this means: "I desire mercy, not sacrifice." For I have not come to call the righteous, but sinners'" (Matt. 9:10-13).

We must be challenged by these words from Jesus: "Go and learn." Learning is found in the going. The fruit of wrestling with Kingdom worship and justice will never be harvested by theorizing or sitting still.

Jesus' critics are puzzled by His seemingly reckless, irresponsible behavior, especially so early in His ministry. Why start like this, eating with "sinners"? What kind of reputation is He building? He won't get any respect by being seen with the likes of *these* people . . . What is He up to?

Jesus gives a profound answer to these questions: You really want to know why I do what I do? You really want to know what makes me tick . . . what motivates me . . . what moves me? *Do you?* Then take my advice: *Go* . . . yes, go and learn what this means, because you can't get it out of a book or a lecture or the best DVD series on the market. You can't learn who I am without getting up and moving out of your comfort and safety zones. *Go* . . . go and learn what this means: "I desire mercy, not sacrifice."

Quoting from Hosea 6:6 (another passage about discovering worship that is acceptable to God), Jesus challenges us to embrace mercy that is beyond sacrifice. The point is not how much I give, how generous I am, or how sacrificial my works of service are. The point is mercy. Did I learn to love?

As Mother Teresa says:

I am not sure exactly what heaven will be like, but I do know that when we die and it comes time for God to judge us, He will *not* ask, "How many good things have you done in your life?" Rather, He will ask, "How much *love* did you put into what you did?"[2]

I have purposely kept this book close to home. It is the place to begin: Not looking to a faraway place, or another city or even another neighborhood to experience the fragrance of justice, but instead allowing the Holy Spirit to heal our sight so that we can see where there is a need to set things right—to do justice—right around us.

I trust that the words and words spilled out on these pages will be inspiration as well as invitation. At the very least, I pray that they will prompt you to wrestle through Scripture with the teachings of Jesus and the lifestyles of the earliest Christian community that fused worship with justice. And if my musings launch you into a life's quest to unlock the fragrance of justice in all spheres of life, beginning where you live, I will consider both of us truly blessed.

The following are a few pointers for the journey.

Allow the Holy Spirit to awaken dissatisfaction with expressions of worship that are not touched by justice and mercy.

I don't know of any better place to begin than in a posture of humility and dependence on the Holy Spirit. Learn to wait, to listen. For it is only there that *true* sight can be given. Being wrenched free from our smugness, spiritual pride and self-sufficiency can only happen with the help of the Holy Spirit.

> You say, "I am rich; I have acquired wealth and do not need a thing." But you do not realize that you are wretched, pitiful, poor, blind and naked. I counsel you to buy from me gold refined in the fire, so you can become rich; and white clothes to wear, so you can cover your shameful nakedness; and salve to put on your eyes, so you can see (Rev. 3:17-18).

Dependence on the Holy Spirit keeps the whole adventure anchored in a place of worship, yet it creates a restlessness that won't allow the place of worship to be enough. We must go and find Him where He dwells: among the poor, the broken and the marginalized of society, beyond the walls surrounding us, and—at times—beyond the religious systems of the Church itself.

Ask for guidance and inspiration for creative ways to introduce the worshiping community to an encounter with the poor. If you are part of the group responsible for corporate worship, address some aspect of injustice or ministry with the poor in the regular activities of the worship. Make it as much a part of things as rehearsals and planning. You will be amazed at the depth it will bring to your worship expression.

Also remember: Learning is more caught than taught. Motivation through words and instruction will only do so much. It is living it out, taking risks and trying again and again that will truly inspire change.

Keep it simple: Who do you see and what do you have?

One of my mentors, John Wimber, was a key figure in the founding of an international church-planting movement known as the Vineyard. He died some time ago, and I still miss him. Not long before he died, I discovered something about who he was.

Every day, John made sure that there were three things he had along with him. In the trunk of his car, he had two bags: One was filled with groceries and perishables, so that if he encountered someone in need who had access to refrigeration and a place to prepare a meal, he could give them the food. The other bag was filled with dried and canned goods that didn't need refrigeration or a place for preparation so that he could give this to someone in need who had no place to cook. The third item he carried in his wallet: coupons or gift certificates so that he could assist someone who had no place to go and needed to eat on the spot.

Every day. Every single morning, John left the house with this prayer: "Lord, who am I going to see today? Show me the poor."

John planted the Anaheim Vineyard church—which to this day has an extensive mercy ministry in which hundreds are fed each month—but that corporate effort never replaced his personal journey with the poor. His was a lifestyle of worship, and I have often wondered what impact his unseen faithfulness had (and continues to have) on our entire movement.

As Mother Teresa said, "If you can't feed a hundred people, then just feed one." We need to *see* and to give whatever we have in the moment: sometimes a prayer, other times cash, or maybe just a genuine smile. But what we have, we give—and leave the results with God. Even if we are led to establish significant programs and mobilize massive resources on behalf of the poor, we must not stray from the simplicity of a lifestyle of love.

View structures and programs as doorways to friendship.

Structure is critical. Without it, everything sags like a body with no skeleton. Not much movement can take place without that framework. The trick is to remember that structure must serve the organism, not dictate what the organism does. The skeleton does not decide where to walk, how to get there, or who to love along the way.

Nowhere is this more true than in the realm of mercy and justice. When the ball gets rolling, it's amazing how many resources come flowing in: people's consciences are pricked, old closets are cleaned out, and the receipt for that one last tax write-off is put in the file. When the momentum gets going, it is far too easy to roll right past relationship and just pump out the goods.

Another reason structure can get out of hand is that the need is so great. There is always another crisis, always the next person or family in desperate need of help *now*. But we must not be need-driven. If we are, we'll start at one end of the street and never make it to the next block. We must be led by the Holy Spirit into relationship.

In the first inner-city community we led, we committed at the outset to maintain relationship at the center of all we did. Instead of starting a soup kitchen, free store or distribution center, we began by finding people and going to where they were. We brought them food (which was more time-consuming than requiring them to come to a centralized location), which forced us into a relational connection. It also allowed for personal touch to accompany the goods. Eventually, friendships emerged; instead of a program providing for people, *people encountered people*—and everyone was changed on the journey.

I'll never forget the day one of our big freezers was plundered. The "wise" counsel was to lock that thing up and only have a couple of people with keys to prevent another theft, but I remember thinking, *That's what it's there for! If people want the food, let them take it.* There were concerns about how the food would be used (would it be sold for drugs?), but I just could not bring myself to lock up food that was meant for people in need.

Over the long run, this approach paid off. As trust was built in the community, a sense of ownership was cultivated in all of us. The "us vs. them" mentality began to break down, and a sense of oneness developed. In fact, there were several times when items were stolen from our ministry center and then returned when people found out where they had come from. "We don't take from those guys, man . . . take that back. They love us—don't mess with them."

It takes commitment to keep things running this way. Structure fights hard to take over, wooing us with its efficiency and easier way of doing things. But when we distance ourselves from friendship in favor of a system, nobody wins.

Take the Three Steps of encounter.

This is a simple model we've used over the years, and it's a helpful guide for processing encounters with the poor and marginalized.

First Encounter: Assume this encounter is about you, not them.

We need to appreciate the poor as a gift to us. In more ways than we can imagine, we *need* the poor.

There is so much that they can teach the rest of the community and so much that we can learn about ourselves as we encounter their brokenness.

In the first encounter with someone who has been hurt by poverty and/or injustice, we need to assume that the connection is about *our* change, not about fixing *them*. Give them that 20 bucks or whatever you have and don't worry about what they're going to do with it. This is about your heart, not their lifestyle.

What stereotypes kick in that need to change? What aspects of prejudice and racism are triggered in this encounter? How much do we cling to our material goods in the face of need? How grasping and selfish are we, really?

As we ask these questions, we discover darkness lurking inside us that we didn't even know was there. We discover—as we saw in the Revelation 3 passage—that *we* are the poor, the wretched, the naked and the blind, and that many times we are more in need of a touch from God than those we think we're helping.

Second Encounter: Assume this encounter will lead to relationship.

Be ready for a second encounter. Maybe it's someone

you bumped into on your way to work—they were on the street as you were walking or on a corner as you drove by. Maybe it's someone in your neighborhood, or someone you met at an event or a program organized by the church you attend. However the first encounter happened, don't be surprised if you see that person again (and again).

Now that you've made their acquaintance, you can take the initiative. Approach them and see how they're doing. Ask them how their week was. Let them know you prayed for them (only if you did, of course!) and that you're interested in who they are.

"Let's not make it about money this time," you can say. "Let's go grab coffee (on me) and get to know each other."

There may be rejection, but don't be surprised if there is a connection! It may take several meetings with each other for a bridge to be built, but make friendship your goal over a quick fix or easy solution. And then see where it goes.

Third Encounter: Allow friendship to develop.
The third encounter is really everything beyond the first two encounters. Somewhere along the way, if you walk long enough with a person, true friendship can

and probably will develop. It's in friendship that topics of lifestyle and life choices can be addressed with authority and staying power. You've gone beyond program; it's now one friend helping another. The journey can take a new (and giant) step forward.

A give-and-take begins to happen, as well. The sharing of story and space makes life a cooperative effort rather than a one-way charity case. *That* is true friendship.

Allow your vision to broaden.

Educate yourself about poverty and injustice beyond stereotypes, simplistic explanations and what you've heard. There is so much we do not know. There is always more to a person's story than we see at first glance.

Often, some injustice in the past has shattered a person's world and propelled them to a present of poverty and marginalization. This is not an excuse to embrace a victim mentality. It is perspective. It is *sight*.

Broadening your vision is not education through the media, books or seminars. It demands an encounter with flesh and blood. It entails listening more than talking and walking *with* more than reaching *out*. It carries a price tag on all our resources—time, money and emotion—but the challenge of Jesus stands: "Go and learn."

Remember that journey into justice is a journey into community.

From a Kingdom perspective, the poor are at the center of the community—not on the margins. In the Kingdom family, the poor have as much to contribute as everyone else. In Kingdom community, the poor are included in the worshiping Church—not distanced from it. In Kingdom life, there is no integrity to the expression of individual and corporate worship if the poor are ignored (*insulted*, as James says) and injustice brushed aside.

Give voice to the voiceless.

Space must be given for the marginalized to express themselves as part of the community's liturgy and worship. This does not mean equal time given out of a sense of obligation; that would be tokenism (at best), and nothing kills a heart of justice more quickly than guilt. But space must be made at the table for everyone.

In one of the communities we led, we had a significant number of First Nations people with us. We included foods indigenous to their various tribes in our feasts and in feeding the hungry. Over time, we learned some of the different tribal dialects and wrote songs in these languages. We even adjusted some of our "oldies" to include a few words in Native tongues. Eventually, many Native people were comfortable enough to wear their traditional ceremonial dress to our gatherings. These adjustments did not take over or dominate in any way, but dignity and honor were deeply felt and appreciated and we were all richer for the inclusion of diverse stories and worldviews.

We also made room for expressing the pain and anger of an oppressed people group and spent hours and hours praying, crying and reconciling with those affected. We educated ourselves about the injustices that had been suffered and positioned ourselves to address the issues when we could and when appropriate. Our community was stronger because of this commitment.

It's a commitment I still keep today in my adventures inside and outside of North America. Seeking to give voice to those who are seldom heard, I carry various indigenous instruments with me to lead worship all over the world. For me, far from trying to be "cool" or embrace a World Music vibe, it is an issue of justice, of giving voice to the marginalized and poor *of* the earth in the sounds of worship *on* the earth.

Give care to how you communicate.

Words have impact, and language is a justice issue. "In Christ's family there can be no division into Jew and non-Jew, slave and free, male and female. Among us you are all equal. That is, we are all in a common relationship with Jesus Christ" (Gal. 3:28, *THE MESSAGE*).

We must realize that those who have been oppressed or marginalized will be sensitive to the power of words and the way things are communicated. Without advocating a carte blanche political correctness, I believe it is important that in Christian community, we weigh our words very carefully. This is especially important in our public gatherings and places of liturgy.

Something as simple as adjusting "ministry *to* the poor" to "ministry *with* the poor" can have huge ramifications. Or it may be important to shift the word "son" to "child" or "man" to "people" in our worship songs. There must be safety and maturity cultivated across community, and making these changes should never be about our rights. We must prayerfully consider where our language creates more pain than healing and adjust where needed. We must be sensitive to the need for inclusive language and inclusive images in the expression of our liturgy. This is especially critical in urban contexts, where the tensions between cultures are often increased.

Keep an eternal perspective.

The hard work of cultivating a lifestyle of worship and building communities of faith where worship and justice kiss demands an eternal perspective. All we give ourselves to on this side of heaven will only find full consummation in the return of Christ. On this side, we will always have the poor with us; it is in the future age that we will see all injustice banished forever.

Until then, we must wait for God where He already is. As Bono stated in his speech at the 2006 National Prayer Breakfast:

> I mean, God may well be with us in our mansions on the hill. I hope so. He may well be with us as in all manner of controversial stuff. Maybe, maybe not. But the one thing we can all agree, all faiths and ideologies, is that God is with the vulnerable and poor.

God is in the slums, in the cardboard boxes where the poor play house. God is in the silence of a mother who has infected her child with a virus that will end both their lives. God is in the cries heard under the rubble of war. God is in the debris of wasted opportunity and lives, and God is with us if we are with them.[3]

We bow down, lay our crowns at Christ's feet, and follow this righteous, just King wherever His Spirit leads. We trust fully in His perfect vengeance and long for His never-ending reign of peace.

Sitting in a dungeon, facing imminent death, the apostle Paul penned these words:

For I am already being poured out like a drink offering, and the time has come for my departure. I have fought the good fight, I have finished the race, I have kept the faith. Now there is in store for me the crown of righteousness, which the Lord, the righteous Judge, will award to me on that day—and not only to me, but also to all who have longed for his appearing (2 Tim. 4:6-8).

Paul was able to see past the temporal injustices and indignities he had suffered and into the future. He had run the race that was set before him, the conflict had been waged, and all that remained was for a crown to be placed on his head. It was the crown of righteousness, or—if you remember the synonym of "righteousness"—the crown of *justice*.

And this crown awaits everyone who longs for the appearance of Christ, who will bring ultimate justice. Kneeling before the great King of Righteousness, justice will crown our heads as we enter that place of eternal peace and worship.

> Then I saw a new heaven and a new earth, for the first heaven and the first earth had passed away, and there was no longer any sea. I saw the Holy City, the new Jerusalem, coming down out of heaven from God, prepared as a bride beautifully dressed for her husband. And I heard a loud voice from the throne saying, "Now the dwelling of God is with men, and he will live with them. They will be his people, and God himself will be with them and be their God. He will wipe every tear from their eyes. There will be no more death or mourning or

crying or pain, for the old order of things has
passed away" (Rev. 21:1-4).

Let the Kingdom come.
Let worship and justice kiss.

Notes

1. Sheryl A. Kujawa-Holbrook, "Beyond Outreach: Worship, Justice,
   and Radical Hospitality," *The Congregation*, Public Broadcasting
   Service. http://www.pbs.org/thecongregation/indepth/beyond
   outreach.html (accessed March 26, 2006).

2. Mother Teresa, quoted at Wikiquote. http://en.wikiquote.org/wiki/
   Mother_Teresa (accessed April 1, 2006).

3. Bono, "Bono's Remarks to the National Prayer Breakfast," speech given
   February 2, 2006, at the National Prayer Breakfast in Washington,
   D.C., DATA.org. http://www.data.org/archives/000774.php (accessed
   March 26, 2006).

ABOUT THE AUTHOR

David Ruis, along with his wife, Anita, has been involved in church planting and leading worship for several years. David has published several worship songs, including "You're Worthy of My Praise" and "Every Move I Make." David is currently giving significant focus to music and the creative aspects of his calling, including music production, writing and composition. David continues to travel internationally, both speaking and leading worship across denominational lines. He lives with his wife and four children in Los Angeles, California.

The seeds for *The Justice God Is Seeking* were planted when David wrote his first book, *The Worship God is Seeking*, in 2005. To continue the conversation of this book virtually, please visit David Ruis's Los Angeles church community online at www.basileacommunity.com.

Also Available in the Best-Selling Worship Series

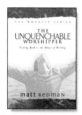

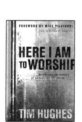
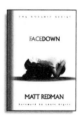

Also Available in the
Best-Selling Worship Series

Inside, Out Worship
Insights for Passionate and
Purposeful Worship
Matt Redman and Friends
ISBN 08307.37103

For the Audience of One
Worshiping the One and Only
in Everything You Do
Mike Pilavachi
ISBN 08307.37049

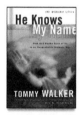

He Knows My Name
How God Knows Each of Us in
an Unspeakably Intimate Way
Tommy Walker
ISBN 08307.36360

Songs from Heaven
Release the Song That God
Has Placed in Your Heart
Tommy Walker
ISBN 08307.37839

Also Available in the Best-Selling Worship Series

The Worship God Is Seeking
An Exploration of Worship
and the Kingdom of God
David Ruis
ISBN 08307.36921

Blessed be Your Name
Worshipping God on the
Road Marked With Suffering
Matt & Beth Redman
ISBN 08307.38193

Breakthrough
How to Experience God's
Presence When You Need
It Most
Tommy Walker
ISBN 08307.39149

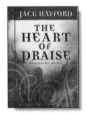

The Justice God Is Seeking
Responding to the Heart of God
Through Compassionate Worship
David Ruis
ISBN 08307.41976

The Heart of Praise
Worship After God's
Own Heart
Jack Hayford
ISBN 08307.37855